SOFTWARE PROJECT MANAGEMENT

T. Anitha | Raghi K.R. | S. Vignesh

KHANNA BOOK PUBLISHING CO. (P) Ltd.
4C/4344, Ansari Road, Darya Ganj, New Delhi, India

Sathyabama Institute of Science and Technology
Jeppiaar Nagar, Rajiv Gandhi Salai, Chennai, Tamilnadu, India

Dear Readers,

To prevent the piracy, this book is secured with HIGH SECURITY HOLOGRAM on the front title cover. In case you don't find the hologram on the front cover title, please write us to at contact@khannabooks.com or whatsapp us at +91-99109 09320 and avail special gift voucher for yourself.

Specimen of Hologram on front Cover title:

Moreover, there is a SPECIAL DISCOUNT COUPON for you with EVERY HOLOGRAM.

How to avail this SPECIAL DISCOUNT:

Step 1: Scratch the hologram
Step 2: Under the scratch area, your "coupon code" is available
Step 3: Logon to www.khannabooks.com
Step 4: Use your "coupon code" in the shopping cart and get your copy at a special discount
Step 5: Enjoy your reading!

Thanks,
Khanna Publishing House

ISBN: 978-93-55388-57-5

Software Project Management
by **T. Anitha, Raghi K.R., S. Vignesh**

First Edition: 2025
Reprint: 2026

To view complete list of books, please scan the QR Code:

Published by:
Khanna Book Publishing Co. (P) Ltd.
CIN: U22110DL1998PTC095547

Visit us at: www.khannabooks.com
Write us at: contact@khannabooks.com

Printed in Bharat.

Preface

Software Project Management integrates the principles of management with the expertise of software engineering. As the demand for robust and efficient software systems grows, the need for effective management practices has never been more essential. This book is designed to equip students and professionals with the knowledge and tools to navigate the complexities of managing software projects, ensuring that they are completed on time, within budget, and to the required standards of quality. The field of software project management is multifaceted, encompassing various aspects ranging from initial project planning and estimation to monitoring progress and controlling risks. This book explores the fundamental principles of managing software projects, focusing on the responsibilities of the project manager, methodologies for estimating effort, and strategies for managing project risks and resources. Topics such as activity planning, monitoring, software quality, and team dynamics are covered in detail, providing a comprehensive guide for anyone involved in the software development lifecycle.

The objective of this book is to help readers understand the nuances of managing software projects and foster a deep understanding of the methodologies and techniques used to ensure successful project execution. The lessons and concepts presented here are intended to be practical, providing readers with tools they can apply to real-world software projects. Throughout the text, the importance of teamwork, leadership, and communication is emphasized, recognizing that effective project management goes beyond technical expertise and requires a balanced approach that considers both human and technological factors.

By the end of this book, readers will be able to apply project management concepts to IT projects, identify potential risks and challenges, and effectively manage the various stages of a software project. Whether serving as a project manager, team leader, or team member, the skills and techniques discussed will enhance the ability to contribute to the success of software projects in any organizational context.

This book is intended as a valuable resource for those eager to master the art of software project management and contribute to the successful delivery of high-quality software products.

Contents

UNIT 1

Introduction to Software Project Management

RATIONALE

Software Project Management (SPM) is essential for ensuring successful software development by efficiently planning, executing, and controlling projects. It covers key activities such as project categorization, evaluation, risk assessment, and resource management. Understanding methodologies, cost-benefit analysis, and portfolio management helps in making informed decisions and optimizing project outcomes. This unit provides a structured approach to handling complex software projects, enhancing efficiency, reducing risks, and ensuring timely delivery. By mastering SPM principles, learners develop the ability to manage multiple projects effectively, align them with business goals, and allocate resources efficiently.

OUTCOMES

- Understand the fundamentals of Software Project Management.
- Identify key activities and methodologies involved in managing software projects.
- Evaluate projects using cost-benefit analysis and risk assessment techniques.
- Gain insights into programme and portfolio management.
- Learn effective resource allocation strategies within programme management.
- Develop skills for strategic project planning and execution.

1.1 INTRODUCTION TO SOFTWARE PROJECT MANAGEMENT

Software is said to be instructions (computer programs) that when executed provide desired features, function and performance. Data structures enable the programs to adequately manipulate information. Documents describe the operation and use of the programs. Software is a program that is the product of a project. Project is a specific plan or design. Project is a planned undertaking/activity. Project is a large undertaking e.g. a public works scheme.

For example: Unique process, consisting of a set of coordinated and controlled activities with start and finish dates, undertaken to achieve an objective conforming to specific requirements, including constraints of time, cost and resources'. BSO ISO 10006: 1997. Project determines how to carry out a task before starting the task. Project is a new endeavor to accomplish a unique purpose. In the broadest sense, a project is a specific, finite task to be accomplished. Any activity results in a deliverable or a product. Projects always begin with a problem. The project is to provide the solution to this problem. When the project is finished it must be evaluated to determine whether it satisfies the objectives and goals.

Jobs versus Projects

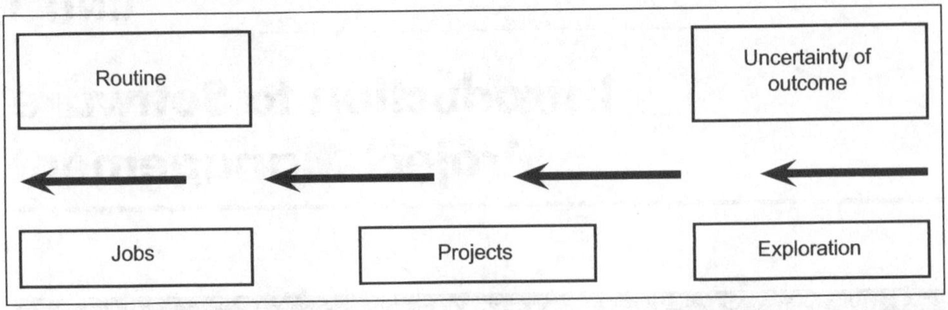

Figure 1.1.

Jobs is a repetition of very well-defined and well understood tasks with very little uncertainty. Projects is in the middle and Exploration is the outcome is very uncertain.

E.g. finding a cure for cancer. There are repetitive jobs a similar task is carried out repeatedly, for example Kwik fit replacing a tired on a car or a lecturer giving an introductory talk on project management. The task is well-defined and there is little uncertainty. In some organizations, software development might tend to be like this in these environments software process management might be important than software project management.

Why is Project Management Important?

Large amounts of money are spent on ICT e.g. UK government in 2003-4 spent £2.3 billions on contracts for ICT and only £1.4 billions on road building Project fail standish Group claim only a third of ICT projects are successful. 82% were late and 43% exceeded their budget.Poor project management a major factor in these failures.

Software Project Management

Software project management is the art and science of planning and leading software projects. It is a sub-discipline of project management in which software projects are planned, monitored and controlled.

Are Software Projects Really Different from Other Projects?

- **Invisibility:** Software can't be rep-resented with geometric models. When a physical object such as a bridge or road is constructed, the progress made can be seen. With Software, progress is not immediately visible. One way of perceiving software project management is as the process of making visible that which is invisible.
- **Complexity:** The proposed model is based on the widely known and accepted. Per dollar, pound or euro spent, software products contain more complexity than other engineered artifacts.
- **Conformity:** The controlling document for software. The traditional' engineer is working with physical systems and physical materials like cement and steel. These physical systems can have some complexity, but are governed by physical laws that are consistent. Software developers have to conform to the requirements of human clients. It is not that individual can be inconsistent.

- **Flexibility:** project management performance. The ease with which software can be changed is seen as one of its strengths. This means that where the software system interfaces with a physical or organizational system, it is expected, where necessary, the software will change to accommodate the other components rather than vice versa. This means the software systems are subject to a high degree of change.

Contract Management versus Technical Project Management

Projects can be:

- **In-house:** clients and developers are employed by the same organization.
- **Out-sourced:** clients and developers employed by different organizations.

Project manager could be contract manager in the client organization and a technical project manager in the supplier/services organization.

1.2 ACTIVITIES COVERED BY SOFTWARE PROJECT MANAGEMENT

Feasibility Study

Is project technically feasible and worthwhile from a business point of view? Whether a prospective project can be started? Gather the information about the requirements of the proposed system. Identify the probable development and operational costs of the system. Estimate the benefits of the new system. Evaluate with a strategic plan with the proper identification of development tasks prioritized. Feasibility study' put as the first stage of development life cycle, and indeed it might be. The recommendation of the feasibility study might be not to carry out the proposed project. Planning of the project should take place after the feasibility study. Clearly the feasibility study itself might need a plan.

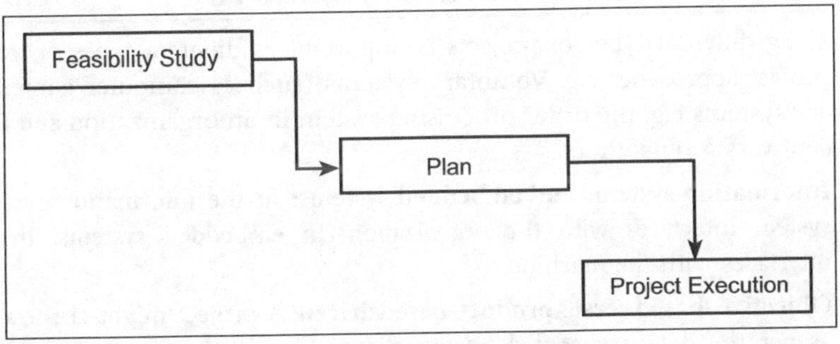

Figure 1.2.

1.3 PLANS AND METHODS AND METHODOLOGIES

Planning

Only done if project is feasible. Formulate an outline plan for the whole project. Detailed plan for the initial stage of the project. Develop detailed planning for the rest of the phases as and when they arise. All plans are to some extent provisional and subject to change. The key point is that the evolving plan allows us to control the project.

Project Execution

Implement plan, but plan may be changed as we go along the project.

A Plan for an activity must be based on some idea of a method of work. A method relates to a type of activity. Plan takes that method and coverts it to real activities and identifying for each activity its start and end dates, who will carry it out, what tools and materials will be used. Groups of methods or techniques are referred to as methodologies.

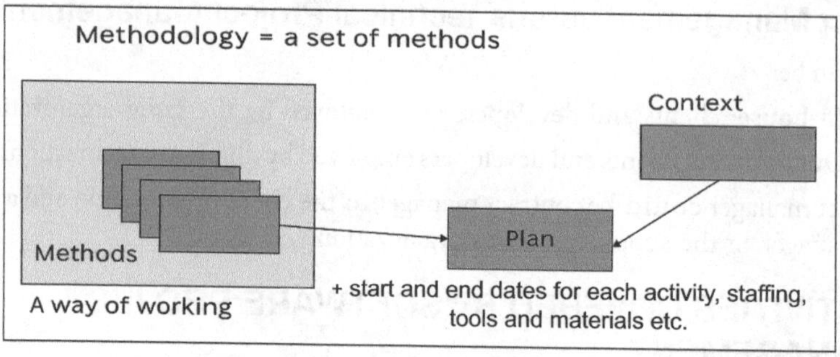

Figure 1.3.

While a method relates to a type of activity in general, a plan takes one or more methods and converts them into real activities by identifying:

- Start and end dates
- Who will carry it out

What tools and materials would be needed?

A methodology is a set of related methods. Methodology' ought to mean the study of methods.

1.4 CATEGORIZING SOFTWARE PROJECTS

Distinguishing different types of projects is important as different types of tasks need different project approaches e.g. Voluntary systems (such as computer games) versus compulsory systems e.g. the order processing system in an organization and Product-development versus outsourced.

- **Information systems and embedded systems:** In the information systems, the system interfaces with the organization. In embedded systems, the system interfaces with the machine
- **Objective-based versus product-based driven:** A project might create a product as per the details specified by the client. The client has the responsibility for justifying the product.
- **Open versus closed systems:** Open systems are those that interact with the environment and are affected by outside changes. Closed systems are an isolated system that has no interaction with its external environment.

With objective-based projects, a general objective or problem is defined, and there are several different ways in which that objective could be reached. The project team have freedom to select what appears to be the most appropriate approach. With product-based projects, the product is already very strictly defined and the development team's job is to implement the specification with which they have been presented. Information systems projects are more objective-based than is the case with software engineering. In many cases, an objective-based project could consider a problem and recommend a solution that is then implemented by a product-based project.

Problems with software Projects

- Poor estimates and plan
- Lack of quality standards
- Lack of guidance about making organizational decision
- Lack of techniques to make progress visible
- Poor role definition – who does what?
- Incorrect success criteria.

Stakeholders

Stakeholder is persons who have a stake/interest in the project. Stakeholders can be individuals working on a project, groups of people or organizations, or segments of a population. A stakeholder may be actively involved in a project's work, affected by the project's outcome, or in a position to affect the project's success. Stakeholders can be an internal part of a project's organization, or external, such as customers, creditors, unions, or members of a community. Internal to the project team. They are under the direct control of the project leader. External to the project team, but within the same organization. The persons involved in providing assistance from other sources to carry out the system's testing and functionality. External to both the project team and the organization. Customers and investors will benefit from the system or the sub-contractors who will carry out work for the project. Different stakeholders may have different objectives need to define common project objectives. Each stakeholder will have their own goals and concerns in relation to the project which may be different from those of the project as a whole. For example, a software developer might work to make a living, pay the mortgage, learn new things, and solve interesting problems. The main stakeholders need to understand and accept overall project objectives that everyone can agree to.

Setting Objectives

The project details should be clearly defined that are accepted by all the employees of an organization. The project authority must be identified where there is more than one group. Need for a project authority, sets the project scope, allocates/approves costs.

This authority is held by a project steering committee that has the overall responsibility for setting, monitoring and modifying the objectives.

Could be one person or a group

- Project Board
- Project Management Board
- Steering committee

Different people who are involved in a project (Stakeholders) will have different interests in the project and are likely to see different outcomes as important.

For example, end-users would want a system that is user-friendly', that is, easy to learn and to use, and a system that helps rather than hinders them from doing their jobs. Their managers may be more interested in whether the new system would allow them to reduce staffing levels.It is important that a set of clearly defined objectives are identified and published for the project. Some individual or group needs to be pinpointed who acts as the main client for the project. Informally, the objective of a project can be defined by completing the statement:

The project will be regarded as a success if.........

Rather like post-conditions for the project.

Focus on what will be put in place, rather than how activities will be carried out. The focus here needs to be on what the situation will be when the project is completed. In what ways will the world be different? The objectives should avoid describing activities:

e.g. a new payroll application will be operational by 4th April not design and code a new payroll application

Objectives should be SMART

S – Specific, that is, concrete and well-defined

M – Measurable, that is, satisfaction of the objective can be objectively judged

A – Achievable, that is, it is within the power of the individual or group concerned to meet the target

R – Relevant, the objective must relevant to the true purpose of the project

T – Time constrained: there is defined point in time by which the objective should be achieved.

Goals/sub-objectives

These are steps along the way to achieving the objective. Informally, these can be defined by completing the sentence...

Objective X will be achieved

If the following goals are all achieved A.............B............. C etc.

Scoring a goal in football is a goal' or sub-objective on the way to achieving the overall objective of winning the match. Sub-objectives and objectives can be nested in a hierarchy, so that the objective of winning the match could itself be a goal or sub-objective on the way to winning the league etc.

A goal can be allocated to an individual. Individual may have the capability of achieving goal, but not the objective on their own e.g.—

- Objective – user satisfaction with software product
- Analyst goal – accurate requirements
- Developer goal – software that is reliable.

Goals can be formulated in such a way that they represent what an individual or group need to do to contribute to the success of the project's objectives.

In the example above, the analyst or developer, by themselves, cannot guarantee user satisfaction. The analyst can contribute to the achievement of the objective by making sure the users' requirements are accurately recorded and the developer by making sure that the software is reliable.

1.5 PROJECT EVALUATION AND PROGRAMME MANAGEMENT

Project evaluation is normally carried out in step 0 of stepwise Project evaluation is a step-by-step process of collecting, recording and organizing information about project results

- **Short:** term outputs (immediate results of activities or project deliverables)
- **Long:** term outputs (changes in behavior, practice or policy resulting from the result.

Management Principles

Management can be defined as all activities and tasks undertaken by one or more persons for the purpose of planning and controlling the activities of others in order to achieve objectives or complete an activity that could not be achieved by others acting independently. Management is to manage to forecast and plan to organize, to command, to co-ordinate and to control. Management is getting things done through the efforts of other people. It is process towards the attainment of desired goals.

This involves the following activities:

- Planning is deciding what is to be done
- Organizing is making arrangements
- Staffing is selecting the right people for the job
- Directing is giving instructions
- Monitoring is checking on progress
- Controlling is taking action to remedy hold-ups
- Innovating is coming up with solutions when problems emerge
- Representing is liaising with clients, users, developers and other stakeholders.

Project Management

Project management is the discipline of planning, organizing, and managing resources to bring about the successful completion of specific projects goals and objectives. A project is a planned undertaking to present results at a specified time. Here undertaking means making new product or changing old product.

Task: A piece of work assigned or done as part of one's duties.

Activity: Activity definition refers to the process of parsing a project into a number of individual tasks which must be completed before the deliverables can be considered completed. Activity definitions rely on a number of specific input processes. Activities can be subdivided into tasks.

Phase: a group of activities/tasks, producing a significant deliverable work product.

Project: A unique, goal-oriented, time-bound and constrained undertaking.

System: an organized element acting as a whole.

Project Planning

- Carried out before development starts.

Important activities:

- Estimation

- Scheduling
- Staffing
- Risk management
- Miscellaneous plans

The project initiation stage, an initial plan is made. As the project start, the project is monitored and controlled to proceed as per the plan. But the initial plan is refined from time to time to factor in additional details and constraints about the project become available.

Traditional versus Modern Project Management

Projects are increasingly based on either tailoring some existing product or reusing certain pre-built libraries. Facilitating and accommodating client feedbacks. Facilitating customer participation in project development work. Incremental delivery of the product with evolving functionalities. Rather than making a long-term project completion plan, the project manager plans all incremental deliveries with evolving functionalities. This type of project management is called Extreme project management.

Management Control

It is a set of policies and procedures designed to keep operations going according to plan||. The management has to know about all the activities of an organization. The local managers may have to collect required data. Data – the raw details. e.g., 6,000 documents processed at location X. "Data processing has to be done so that raw data is transformed into useful information. Information is the data is processed to produce something that is meaningful and useful. e.g., productivity is 100 documents a day". This helps in taking decisions/plans. The project manager has to find out the impact on staff while taking decisions. This results in modeling the consequences of a potential solution. The progress details are to be updated.

Information and Control in Organizations

Hierarchical Information and Control Systems: Larger projects are to have a hierarchical management structure. Management information flows up the organizational structure and control flows down. Project team members will each have a group who allocates them work and to whom they report progress. The group leader will report to a manager at the next higher level. There might be problems that cannot be resolved at a level. They will have to be reported to the next higher level of management.

The information will have to be summarized to avoid overloaded information at the higher levels, levels of decision making and information. Each decision made in a project environment should be based on adequate information. Decisions are grouped at strategic, tactical and operational levels. Strategic decision making is about deciding objectives. Tactical decision making ensures that the objectives are fulfilled. The project leader will have to formulate a plan of action to meet those objectives. The project leader monitors the progress to verify whether the objectives are met ad take necessary action. Operational decisions relate to day–to–day work implementing the project.

- **Modelling:** working out the probable outcomes of various decisions. e.g., if we employ two more staff at location X how quickly can we get the documents processed?
- **Implementation:** carrying out the remedial actions that have been decided upon.

1.6 PROJECT PORTFOLIO MANAGEMENT

A programme is a portfolio comprised of multiple projects that are managed and coordinated as one unit with the objective of achieving (intangible) outcomes and benefits for the organization. Strategic and operational assessment carried by an organization on behalf of customer is called portfolio management [third party developers]. They make use of assessment of any proposed project themselves. They ensure for consistency with the proposed strategic plan. They proposed project will form part of a portfolio of ongoing and planned projects. Selection of projects must take account of possible effects on other projects in the portfolio (example: competition of resource) and the overall portfolio profile (example: specialization versus diversification).

The Business Case

The business case should be established at the time of the project's feasibility study.

The quantification of benefits will require the formulation of a business model which explains how the new application can generate the claimed benefits. Provides a justification for starting the project. Should show that the benefits of the project will exceed development, implementation and operational costs. Needs to take account of business risks. The difference between project success (the project is successfully completed) and business risks (the new product or system successfully established by the project goes on to generate benefits for the organization).

Contents of a business case:

- **Introduction/background:** describes a problem to be solved or an opportunity to be exploited.
- **The proposed project:** a brief outline of the project scope.
- **The market:** the project could be to develop a new product (e.g. a new computer game). The likely demand for the product would need to be assessed.
- **Organizational and operational infrastructure:** How the organization would need to change? This would be important where a new information system application was introduced. Benefits These should be express in financial terms where possible. In the end it is up to the client to assess these as they are going to pay for the project.
- **Outline implementation plan:** how the project is going to be implemented. This should consider the disruption to an organization that a project might cause.
- **Costs:** the implementation plan will supply information to establish it.
- **Financial analysis:** combines costs and benefit data to establish value of project.

Portfolio Management

The concerns of PPM include evaluating proposals for projects , Assessing the risk involved with projects, Deciding how to share resources between projects, Taking account of dependencies between projects, Removing duplication between projects, Checking for gaps

Elements to PPM

1. Project portfolio definition
   - Create a central record of all projects within an organization must decide whether to have ALL projects in the repository or, say, only ICT projects.

- The difference between new product development projects and renewal projects e.g. for process improvement.

2. Project portfolio management

   Actual costing and performance of projects can be recorded and assessed

3. Project portfolio optimization

Information gathered above can be used achieve better balance of projects e.g. some that are risky but very valuable balanced by less risky but less valuable projects. You may want to allow some work to be done outside the portfolio e.g. quick fixes

1.7 EVALUATION OF INDIVIDUAL PROJECTS COST BENEFIT EVALUATION TECHNIQUES

Evaluation of Individual Project

1. Technical Assessment

It is the second criteria for evaluating the project. Technical assessment of a proposed system evaluates functionality against available hardware/software

Hardware/Software

Limitations: Nature of solutions produced by strategic information systems plan Cost of solution. Undergoes cost-benefit analysis.

2. Economic Assessment

Cash–benefit analysis: It is the common way for carrying out the economical assessment. It focuses on whether the estimated income and other benefits exceed the estimated costs.

It comprises of two steps: Identifying and estimating all the cost and benefits of carrying out the project and operating the delivered application.

- **Development costs:** Development costs include the salaries and other employment costs of the staff involved in the development project and all associated costs.
- **Set-up:** Setup costs include the costs of putting the system into place. These consists of the costs of the new hardware
- **Operational costs:** It consists of the costs of operating the system once it has been installed. Expressing these costs and benefits in common units.

Cash Flow Forecasting

As important as estimating the overall costs and benefits of a project is the forecasting of the cash flow that will take place and their timing. A cash flow forecast will indicate when expenditure and income will take place. The following diagram shows typical product/System life cycle cash flow. We need to spend money, such as staff wages during the development stages of a project. Such expenditure cannot be deferred until is received. It is important that we know that we can fund the development expenditure either from the company's own resources or by borrowing from the bank. The timing of costs and income for a product of system needs to be estimated. The development of the project will incur costs. When the system or product is released, it will generate income that gradually pays off costs. Some costs may relate to decommissioning think of demolishing a nuclear power station.

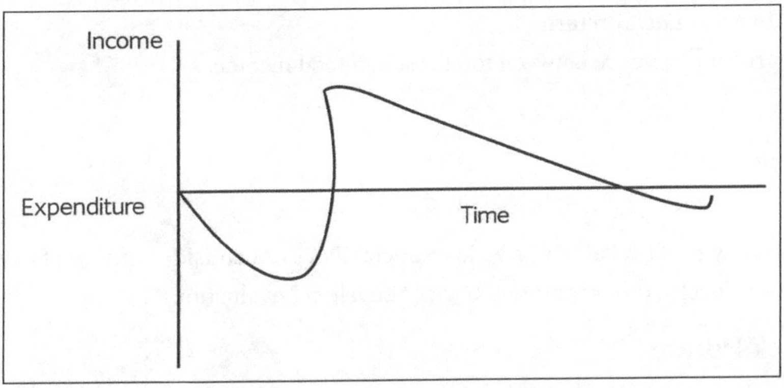

Figure 1.4.

Year	Cash-flow
0	-100,000
1	10,000
2	10,000
3	10,000
4	20,000
5	100,000
Net profit	50,000

Year 0 represents all the costs before system is operation and Cash-flow is value of income less outgoing, Net profit value of all the cash-flows for the lifetime of the application.

Table: Project Cash Flow Projections

In any t, it is vital to have some forecast of when expenditure such as the payment of salaries and bank interest will take place and when any income is to be expected, such as payment on completion or possibly, stage payments. Accurate cash flow forecasting is not easy, as it needs to be done early in the project life cycle and many items to be estimated. The following table illustrates cash flow forecasts for a project. In each case it is assumed that the cash flows take at the end of each year. For short term projects or where candidates' projects demonstrate significant seasonal cash flow patterns it can be advisable to produce quarterly, or monthly, cash flow forecasts.

Cost-Benefits Evaluation Techniques

Various cost-benefits Evaluation Techniques are

- Net profit
- Payback period

- Return on investment
- Net present value
- Internal rate of return

Net profit: Difference between total cost and total income.

Pros

Easy to calculate

Cons

Does not show profit relative to size investment, Does not consider timing of payments

Not very useful other than for "back of envelope" evaluations

Payback Period

The payback measures the length of time it takes a company to recover in cash its initial investment. The length of time it takes the project to generate cash equal to the investment and pay the company back. It is calculated by dividing the capital investment by the net annual cash flow. This is the time it takes to start generating a surplus of income over outgoings. What would it be below? If the net annual cash flow is not expected to be the same, the average of the net annual cash flows may be used. The payback period is the time taken to recover the initial investment. Or is the length of time required for cumulative incoming returns to equal the cumulative costs of an investment.

Cash Payback Period = Capital Investment/Average annual net cash flow Year 1:10,000

Year 2: 10,000

Year 3: 10,000

Year 4: 20,000

Year 5: 1,00,000

10,000 + 10,000 + 10,000 + 20,000 + 1,00,000 = 1,50,000

The payback period for the project is years 5. The shorter the payback period, the sooner the company recovers its cash investment. When net annual cash flows are different, the cumulative net annual cash flows are used to determine the payback period.

The payback period would be about 4.5 years. This can be calculated as the last year in which the accumulated cash flow was negative + (absolute accumulated cash flow at the end of that year / cash-flow for the next year) e.g. year 4 + (50,000/100,000). This assumes that the flow of cash is constant throughout the year in question e.g. £100,000/12 or £8,333 a month in year 5.

Return On Investment (ROI)

It provides a way of comparing the net profitability to the investment required. Or a performance measure used to evaluate the efficiency of an investment or to compare the efficiency of a number of different investments.

Disadvantages: It takes no account of the timing of the cash flows.

Rate of returns bears no relationship to the interest rates offered or changed by bank.

average annual profit = net profit / total no. of years

ROI = (average annual profit * 100) / total investment

average annual profit = 50,000/5 = 10,000 ROI = 10,000/100,000 × 100 = 10%

Net Present Value (NPV)

A project evaluation technique takes into account the profitability of a project and the timing of the cash flows that are produced. Sum of all incoming and outgoing payments, discounted using an interest rate, to a fixed point in time (the present). It is a discounted cash flow technique. Would you rather I gave you £100 today or in 12 months' time? If I gave you £100 now you could put it in savings account and get interest on it. If the interest rate was 10% how much would I have to invest to get £100 in a year's time?

Figure is the net present value of £100 in one year's time. If you invested £91 you would get £9.10 in interest which would give you £100.10 in 12 months. The interest rate of 10% is used purely to make it easy to do the calculations, not because it is a realistic rate.

Consider the timing and amount of cash flows. To use the net present value method, you will need to know the cash inflows, the cash outflows, and the company's required rate of return on its investments. The required rate of return becomes the discount rate used in the NPV calculation.

Discount Factor

$$\text{Discount factor} = 1/(1+r)t$$

r is the interest rate (e.g. 10% is 0.10)

t is the number of years

In the case of 10% rate and one year Discount factor = 1/(1 + 0.10) = 0.9091. In the case of 10% rate and two years

Discount factor = 1/(1.10 × 1.10) = 0.8294 In the case of 10% rate and three years

Discount factor = 1/(1.10 × 1.10 × 1.10) = 0.7513 In the case of 10% rate and four years

Discount factor = 1/(1.10 × 1.10 × 1.10 × 1.10) = 0.6830 In the case of 10% rate and five years

Discount factor = 1/(1.10 × 1.10 × 1.10 × 1.10 × 1.10) = 0.6209

Year	Cash-flow	Discount factor	Discounted cash flow
0	- 100,000	1.0000	-100,000
1	10,000	0.9091	9,091
2	10,000	0.8264	8,264
3	10,000	0.7513	7,513
4	20,000	0.6830	13,660
5	100,000	0.6209	62,090
		NPV	618

Discounted cash flows = Cash-flow * Discount factor

NPV is the sum of the discounted cash flows for all the years of the project. (NPV is the lifetime of the completed application is included in the project). Figure of £618 means that £618 more would be made than if the money were invested at 10%. NPV of £0 would be the same amount of profit as would be generated by investing at 10%.

Internal Rate of Return (IRR)

IRR is the discount rate that would produce an NPV of 0 for the project can be used to compare different investment opportunities. There is a Microsoft Excel function which can be used to calculate determines the interest yield of the proposed capital project at which the net present value equals zero, which is where the present value of the net cash inflows equals the investment. If IRR is greater than the company's required rate of return, the project may be accepted. To determine the internal rate of return requires two steps. First, the internal rate of return factor is calculated by dividing the proposed capital investment amount by the net annual cash inflow. Then, the factor is found in the Present Value of an Annuity of 1 table using the service life of the project for the number of periods. The discount rate that the factor is the closest to is IRR. Can be used to compare different investment opportunities

IRR = (rate giving positive NPV)+(difference between rates * (positive NPV/difference between NPV))

Calculate NPV with Discount Factor =10%

Year	Cash-flow	Discount factor	Discounted cash flow
0	-9000	1.0000	-9000
1	2000	0.9091	1818.2
2	3000	0.8264	2479.2
3	3000	0.7513	2253.9
4	4000	0.6830	2732
		NPV	283.3

Calculate NPV with discount factor 12%

Year	Cash-flow	Discount factor	Discounted cash flow
0	-9000	1.0000	-9000
1	2000	0.8928	1785.6
2	3000	0.7971	2391.6
3	3000	0.7117	2135.4
4	4000	0.6355	2542
		NPV	-145.4

IRR =10 + (2*(283.3/(283.3-(-145.4))))

= 10 + (2*(283.3/428.7)) =11.8

1.8 RISK EVALUATION

It deals with uncertainty. Risk evaluation is meant to decide whether to proceed with the project or not, and whether the project is meeting its objectives. When the project exceeds its original specification. Deviations from achieving it objectives and so on. Every project involves risk. The project risks which part the project completed successfully and the business risk that the delivered products are nor profitable. Project A might appear to give a better return than B but could be riskier. Could draw up draw a project risk matrix for each project to assess risks – see next overhead. For riskier projects could use higher discount rates Risk evaluation consists of:

- Risk identification and ranking
- Risk and NPV
- Cost benefit analysis
- Risk profile analysis.

a. Risk Identification and Ranking

Identify the risk and give priority. Could draw up draw a project risk matrix for each project to assess risks. Project risk matrix used to identify and rank the risk of the project.

Example of a project risk matrix:

Risk	Importance	Likelihood
Client rejects proposed look and feel of site	H	—
Competitors undercut prices	H	M
Warehouse unable to deal with increased demand	M	L
Online payment has security problems	M	M
Maintenance costs higher than estimated	L	L
Response times deter purchasers	M	M

In the table Importance relates to the cost of the damage if the risk was to materialize and likelihood to the probability that the risk will actually occurs. Indicates High, M indicates medium and L indicates low.

b. Risk and Net Present Value

Where a project is relatively risky it is common practice to use a higher discount rate to calculate the NPV. The risk premium be an additional 2% for a safe project or 5% for a fairly risky project. Projects may be categorized as high, medium or low risk using a scoring method and risk premiums designated for each category.

c. Cost-benefit Analysis

A rather more sophisticated approach to the evaluation of risk is to consider each possible outcome, probability of its occurring and the corresponding value of the outcome. Rather than a single cash flow forecast for a project, we will then have a set of cash flow forecasts, each with an associated probability of occurring. The value of the project is then obtained by summing of the cost or benefit for each possible outcome weighted by its corresponding probability.

Drawback

Does not take full account of worst-case scenarios. (averaging out the negative and positive outcomes of the scenarios)

Sales	Annual Sales income i	Probability p	Expected value i*p
High	8,00,000	0.1	80,000
Medium	6,50,000	0.6	3,90,000
Low	1,00,000	0.3	30,000
Expected Income			5,00,000

d. Risk Profile Analysis

An approach which attempts to overcome some of the objectives to cost benefit averaging is the construction of risk profiles using sensitivity analysis. It compares the sensitivity of each factor of project profiles by varying parameters which affect the project cost benefits.

E.g.: Vary the original estimates of risk plus or minus 5% and re-calculate the expected b cost benefits. p1 depart far from p2, have large variation. p3 have much profitable than expected. All three projects have the same expected profit.Compare to p2, p1 is less risky.

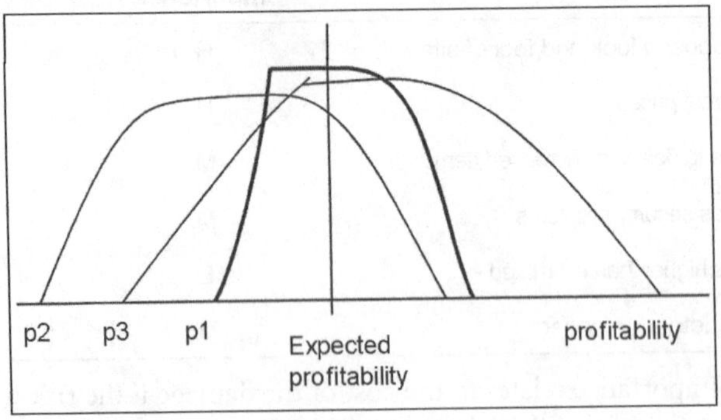

Figure 1.5.

1.9 PROGRAMME MANAGEMENT

A programme as a group of projects that are managed in a co-ordinated way to gain benefits that would not be possible were the projects to be managed independently. A programme is a collection of projects that all contribute to the same overall organization goal. Effective programme management requires that there is a well-defined programme goal and that all the organization's projects are selected and tuned to contribute to this goal Evaluating of project is depends on:

- How it contributes to programme goal.
- It is viability [capability of developing or useful].
- Timing.
- Resourcing - software available to develop projects.

For successful strategic assessment, there should be a strategic plan which defines:

- Organization's objectives.
- Provides context for defining programme.
- Provides context for defining programme goals.
- Provide context for accessing individual project.

In large organization, programme management is taken care by programmer director and programme executive, rather than, project manager, who will be responsible for the strategic assessment of project. Any potential software system will form part of the user organization's overall information system and must be evaluated within the context of existing information system and the organization's information strategy. If a well-defined information system does not exist then the system development and the assessment of project proposals will be based on a more piece meal approach. Piece meal approach is one in which each project individually early in its life cycle.

Types of Programme

1. Strategic
2. Business cycle programmes
3. Infrastructure programmes
4. Research and development programmes
5. Innovative partnerships

1. Strategic

Several projects together implement a single strategy. For example, merging two organizations will involve many different activities e.g. physical re-organization of offices, redesigning the corporate image, merging ICT systems etc. Each of these activities could be project within an overarching programme.

2. Business Cycle Programmes

A portfolio of project that are to take place within a certain time frame e.g. the next financial year.

3. Infrastructure Programmes

In an organization there may be many different ICT-based applications which share the same hardware/software infrastructure.

4. Research and Development Programmes

In a very innovative environment where new products are developed, a range of products could be developed some of which are very speculative and high-risk but very profitable and some will have a lower risk but will return a lower profit. Getting the right balance would be a key to the organization's long term success.

5. Innovative Partnerships

E.g., pre-competitive co-operation to develop new technologies that could be exploited by a whole range of companies.

Programme Managers versus Project Managers

Programme Manager

Many simultaneous projects personal relationship with skilled resources, Optimization of resource use, Projects tend to be seen as similar Project manager, One project at a time, Impersonal relationship with resources, Minimization of demand for resources and Projects tend to be seen as unique.

The programme manager may well have a pool of staff upon which to call. He/she will be concerned with ensuring the best use of staff. e.g., ensuring that staff has regular work with no periods of enforced idleness between project tasks. The project leader would think in terms of need a Java programmer for four weeks' without concerned which specific person it is.

Strategic programmes:

- Based on UK government's Office of Government Commerce (OGC) approach
- Initial planning document is the Programme Mandate describing
  - The new services/capabilities that the programme should deliver
  - How an organization will be improved
  - Fit with existing organizational goals

A programme director appointed a champion (selected by sponsoring group) for the scheme.The programme director should be someone who is in a prominent position in the organization so that the seriousness and commitment of the organization to the programme are made clear. At the IOE Company, the customers' experience of the organization can be very variable and inconsistent. The employee who records the customer's requirements is different from the people who carry out the work and different again from the clerk who deals with accounts. Different maintenance engineers deal with different types of equipment. A business objective might be to present a consistent and uniform interface to the client. This objective might need changes to a number of different systems which until have been largely self-contained. The work to reorganize each individual area might be treated as separate projects, co-ordinated at a higher level as a programme.

Next stages/documents:

- The programme brief: equivalent of a feasibility study: emphasis on costs and benefits
- The vision statement: explains the new capability that the organization will have
- Worth of the programme
- Setting small team
- Program manager
- The blueprint – explains the changes to be made to obtain the new capability
- Business model
- Organization Structure
- Information system, equipment and non-staff requirement
- Data and info requirements
- Cost, performance and service level requirements
- **Benefit Profiles:** Estimate when the expected benefits will sort to realize following the implementation of enhanced capability.
- **Programme Portfolio:** Preliminary list of the projects that the programme will need in order to achieve its objective.
- **Stakeholders map**: Identifying the groups of people with an interest in the projects and its outcome and their interest may be drawn up.
- **Communication Strategy**: Shows how the appropriate information flow between stake holders can be setup and maintained.

1.10 MANAGING THE ALLOCATION OF RESOURCES WITHIN PROGRAMME MANAGEMENT

Dependency Diagrams

It specifies the physical and technical dependencies between projects.

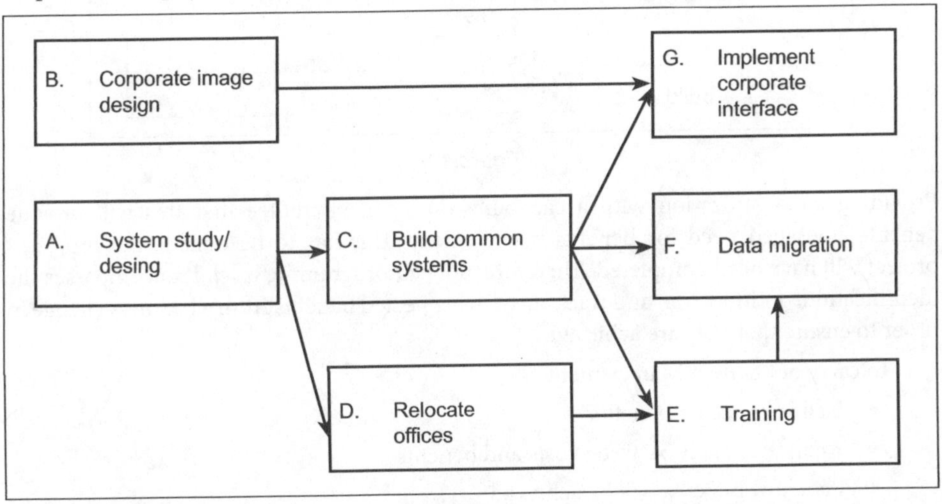

Figure 1.6.

E.g. Dependency diagrams merging of 2 organizations

Delivery Planning

Programme may be subdivided into tranches or identifiable stages. A tranche is group of projects that will deliver their products as one step in the programme. Advantages of Tranche: Deliverables of each of the projects combine to provide a coherent new capability or set of benefits for the client.

Fig. shows an e.g., Delivering tranches of project deliverables.

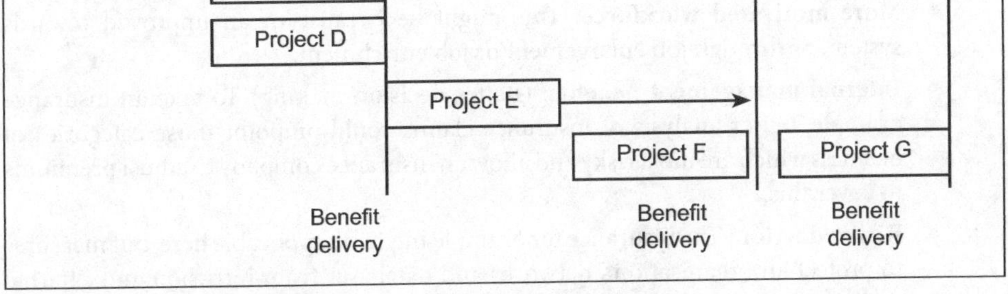

Figure 1.7.

Benefit Management

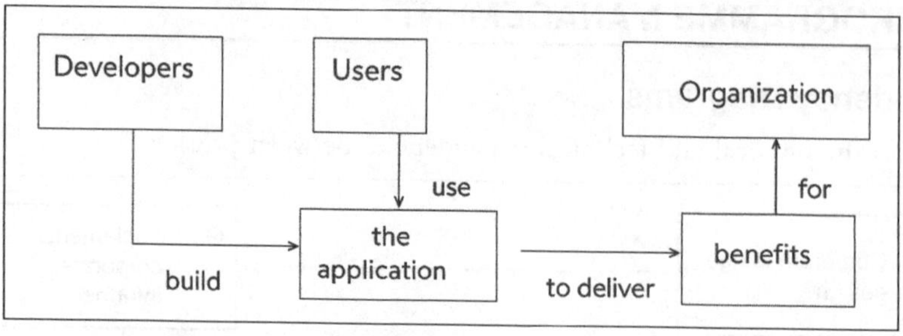

Figure 1.8.

Providing an organization with a capability does not guarantee that this will provide benefits envisaged need for benefits management. This has to be outside the project – project will have been completed. Therefore, done at programme level. It encompasses the identification, optimization and tracking of the expected benefits from a business change in order to ensure that they are achieved.

To carry out benefit Management:

- Define expected benefits
- Analyse balance between costs and benefits
- Plan how benefits will be achieved
- Allocate responsibilities for their achievement
- Monitor achievement of benefits.

Three categories of Benefit:

- **Direct Benefit:** Directly obtained benefit by operating the system.
- **Assessable indirect benefits:** These benefits are obtained due to updation / upgrading the performance of the current system.
- **Intangible benefits:** These benefits are long term, difficult to quantify. It is referred as indirect benefits.

Benefits can be of many different types:

- **Mandatory requirement:** Governmental or European legislation might make certain changes mandatory.
- **Improved quality of service:** For example, an insurance company might want to settle claims by customer more quickly.
- **Increased productivity:** Work can be done at less cost in staff time.
- **More motivated workforce:** This might be because of an improved rewards system, or through job enlargement or job enrichment.
- **Internal management benefits:** (Better decision making) To take an insurance example, better analysis of insurance claims could pinpoint those categories of business which are most risky and allow an insurance company to adjust premiums to cover this.
- **Risk reduction:** The insurance for example might be applicable here, but measures to protect an organisation's networks and databases from intrusion and external malicious attack would be relevant.

- **Economies:** The reduction of cost, other than those related to staff procurement policies might be put in place which encourage the consolidation of purchasing in order to take advantage of bulk buying at discount. Economies' refers to cost-cutting e.g. using an automated telephone system to direct calls without human intervention could allow an organization to reduce staff.
- **Revenue enhancement/acceleration:** E.g., the sooner the bill reaches the customer, the sooner they can pay them.
- **Strategic fit:** A change might not directly benefit a group within the organisation but has to be made in order to obtain some strategic advantage for the organization as the whole.

1.11 AN OVERVIEW OF PROJECT PLANNING

The motivation for identifying an overall framework was that students, and others, were at a loss as to where to start when new to project planning. A structured approach was seen as catering for the needs of such people.

Students are most likely to come into contact with some kind of project planning: when they are involved in student projects, especially those carried in groups and if they are members of a project team when they are undertaking a placement year in industry. The first situation is small-scale compared to the second. The same general principles of planning relate to both. This approach is designed to be applicable to a range of different types of project.

For example, multimedia projects are not explicitly discussed, but one of the authors teaches a course project management for multimedia and the general approach described here seems to work satisfactorily when applied to these types of projects. A project scenario: Bright mouth College Payroll. College currently has payroll processing carried out by a services company. This is very expensive and does not allow detailed analysis of personnel data to be carried out. Decision made to bring payroll in-house' by acquiring an off-the-shelf' application. The use of the off-the-shelf system will require a new, internal, payroll office to be set up. There will be a need to develop some software add-ons. One will take payroll data and combine it with time-table data to calculate the staff costs for each course run in the college. The project manager is Brigette.

Stepwise covers only the planning stages of a project and not monitoring and control

Step 0, It deals with making a decision as to whether a project is worth doing. If so, project evaluation must be done on an individual basis or as part of strategic planning.

Step 1 Identify Project Scope and Objectives

Identify objectives and measures of effectiveness how do we know if we have succeeded? To revise these students could be asked to try to produce a brief statement of the objectives for the student described previously. The student project objectives must be such that a student can realistically be responsible for their achievement.

For instance, an objective to reduce conflict between project team members would be at too high a level for a software developer: he or she is there to produce software and evaluation of the psychometric test would be outside their capabilities. If the student was a psychology student and the project was regarded as a psychological one, then things might be different.

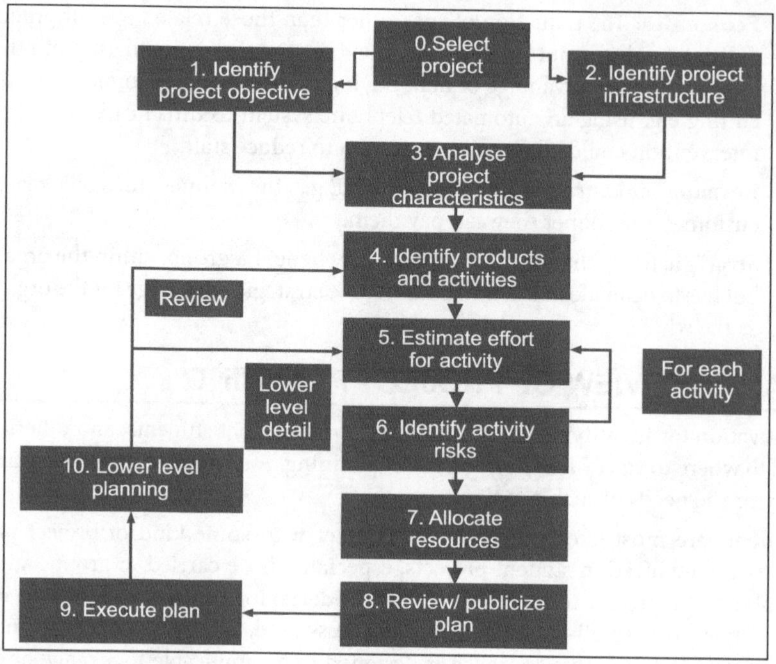

Figure 1.9.

1.2 Establish a project authority a single person or group with unity of purpose to avoid pulled in different directions. In the case of students on placement or carrying final year projects for outside organizations, the problem of identifying who has the final say on the project can occur surprisingly, when different user groups have conflicting requirements. In larger, more formal projects, the project authority might reside in a Project Board or steering committee.

1.3 Identify all stakeholders in the project and their interests who will be affected/ involved in the project? Stakeholders can be anyone who has an interest in the project. They may be users of the final application or might be involved in the development or implementation of the project.

1.4 Modify objectives in the light of stakeholder analysis do we need to do things to win over stakeholders? This is a similar idea to Barry Boehm's Theory 'W' ('W' stands for everyone a winner)

1.5 Establish methods of communication with all parties. how do we keep in contact? including external authorities/providers might lead to making a communications plan.

In the case of a small student project, it might be swapping email addresses and mobile phone numbers. With larger projects, it could involve setting up groups who meet regularly to co-ordinate action. specific communication plans' are drawn up to deal with these issues.

Step 2 Identify Project Infrastructure

Establish link between project and any strategic plan, why did they want the project? Assign priorities to the projects to be carried out. E.g., Hardware and S/W standards. These strategic decisions must be during strategic business plan. Identify installation standards and procedures. What standards do we have to follow Development procedures Document the products created at each stage.

Change Control and Configuration Management Standards

Any changes to requirements are implemented in a safe and orderly way. Quality standards and procedures manual. Quality checks that need to be done at each point of the project life cycle. Measurement programme certain statistics have to collect at various stages of a project. Project Manager should be aware of project planning and control standards.

Identify Project Team Organization

Where do I fit in. Business analyst and software developers are in different group. At the same time as establishing exactly what the project objectives are, the person responsible may know little about the organizational environment in which the application is to be developed and implemented. The actions in Step 2 address this problem. Step 3 Analysis of project characteristics. Step 3 is about examining the nature of the application to be built and the environment in which it is to be built and implemented and identifying the appropriate technical approach. To ensure that appropriate methods are used for the project.

Distinguish the project as either objective or product-based. objective driven will give you more freedom but there is a specified product you have to build to form a solution. With a product-based project the developers have to create a product, the specification of which is clearly defined. In an objective-based project, a problem is defined that needs to be solved but there could be more than one solution.

For example, if an organization needed a payroll application they might consider

(a) writing the system themselves

(b) using a service company to do the payroll for them

(c) acquire an off-the-shelf package

Step 3 Analyse Other Project Characteristics (Including Quality Based Ones)

What is different about this project?

E.g., Information system or Embedded System or safety critical system.

The payroll application is clearly an information system. If an off-the-shelf application is adopted, there is plenty of guidance on how off-the-shelf applications can be accessed and selected that could be consulted by Brigette.

Identify High Level Project Risks

What could go wrong?' what can we do to stop it?' Risk can be attributed to the operational or development environments. Identifying high level risks could influence the general approach to the project. For example, if the users appeared to be uncertain about the precise nature of the requirement then a more iterative approach, including the use of prototypes to refine user needs, might be selected. If the application is very large and complex then breaking it down into increments might be the way to proceed. Back to the scenario: Objectives vs. products. An objective-based approach has been adopted, Some risks. There may not be an off-the-shelf package that caters for the way payroll is processed at

Brightmouth College. Take into account user requirements concerning implementation some organizations (such as government) might require use of the waterfall method

Select general life cycle approach waterfall? Increments? Prototypes?

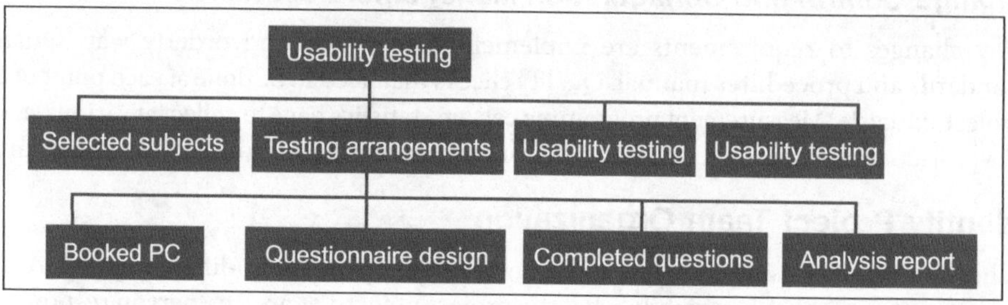

Figure 1.10.

Review overall resource estimates After Risk is identified and project approach is identified, re-estimate the effort and other resources to implement the projected. Function point Estimate does all this increase the cost?

Step 4 Identify Project Products and Activities

Identify and describe project products What do we have to produce? If you were to ask someone to produce, for example, the analysis report in the usability testing scenario, then you would need to explain exactly what you mean by that. This is done via a Product Description. Ds can be re-used from one project to another. A product and the description is relevant to all instances of that product. A specification describes an instance within the class of products. Here we follow the PRINCE approach of firstly identifying the products to be created. These products could be deliverables that will behanded over to the customer or intermediate products such as specifications and design documents that are produced along the way.

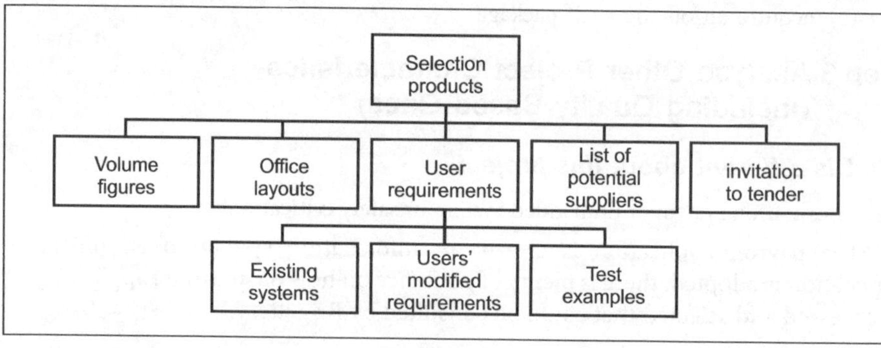

Figure 1.11.

The PBS is a way of listing these products. In the scenario, one set of products will relate to the products needed to produce one or more Invitations To Tender (ITTs) to supply the hardware and software needed to operate the new payroll application. In order to allow the most suitable configuration to be identified the number of transactions and the size of the database needed will have to be identified – volume figures. To set up an appropriate network attached to secure printers and servers, a layout of the proposed office will need to be created. A user requirement will need to be produced which describes the existing system, identifies additional requirements (such as the need to be able to access database details in order to produce one-off queries and reports), and some test data and expected results which further illuminate the details of the requirements. This test data could form the basis of user acceptance tests. A list of potential suppliers to whom ITTs could be sent will be needed, and the actual *ITT* itself which will, among other things, explain how the proposals of potential suppliers are to be submitted.

Document Generic Product Flows

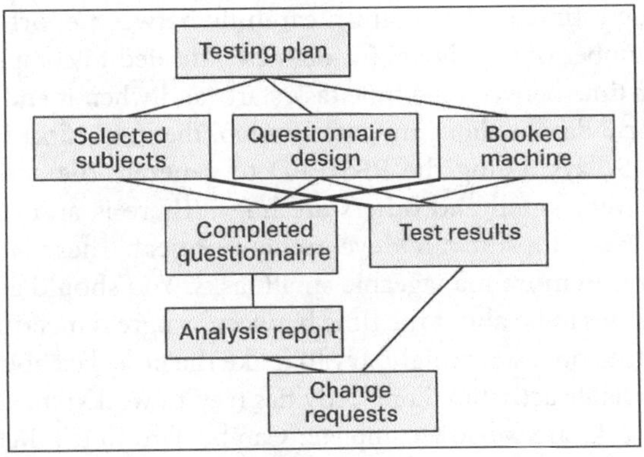

Figure 1.12.

Recognize Product Instances

The Product Breakdown Structure (PBS) and PFD will have identified generic products e.g. software modules' It might possible to identify specific instances e.g. module A', module B'… in many cases this will have to be left to later, more detailed, planning Step 4.4 Produce ideal activity network. Identify the activities needed to create each product in the PFD. More than one activity might be needed to create a single product. Hint: Identify activities by verb + noun but avoid produce…'Draw up activity network. Step 4.5 Add check-points if needed. There are some points in the project when we want to check that the quality of what we have done so far is a sound basis for further work. In the example we have decided to check that all the module designs are compatible with one another before continuing

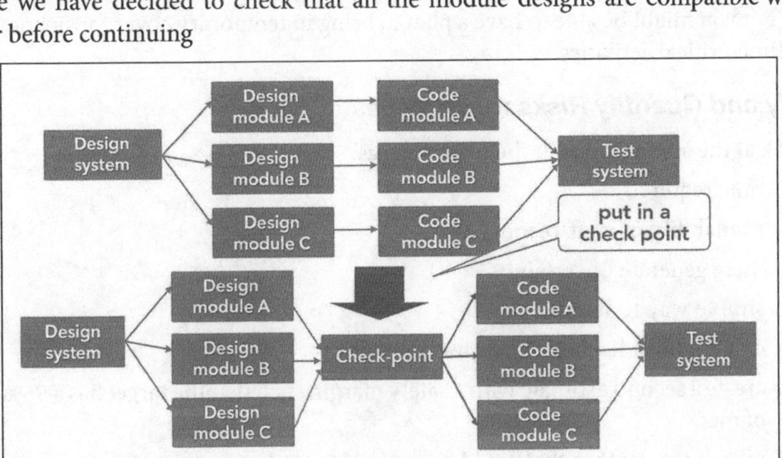

Figure 1.13.

The benefit of reducing wasted work at a later stage when incompatibilities lead to products reworked; has to be balanced against the delay caused by the check-point. The start of coding of modules A, B and C all have to wait for the completion of the design of all the modules A, B and C. With no check-point, module. A could be coded as soon as the design of module A had been done without having to wait for B and C.

Step 5: Estimate Effort for Each Activity

Carry out bottom-up estimates. Distinguish carefully between effort and elapsed time. Effort is the total number of staff-hours (or days etc.) needed to complete a task. Elapsed time is the calendar time between the time task starts and when it ends. If 2 people work on the same task for 5 days without any interruption, then the effort is 10 staff-days and the elapsed time is 5 days. Using the PBS/PFD to generate the activities means that some activities are very small and others are huge. There is an activity called 'write software' which is 70% of a software development project. These large activities need to be broken down into more manageable small tasks. You should aim for the average length of your activities to be about the time between progress meetings e.g. if you have team progress meeting once a fortnight, try to make the tasks last about 2 weeks. Revise plan to create controllable activities. Long activities (say 12 weeks) make a project difficult to control. After 6 weeks are we 50% complete? Can be hard to tell. Better to break down into smaller subtasks.

Conversely, some very short, connected activities might be better bundled together, with a simple checklist. Roughly aim for activities to match the length of the reporting period. If you have progress meetings every 2 weeks, try to identify activities which take two weeks.

Identify Activity Risks

When you produce an estimate for an activity it is worth reflecting about the ts which could cause the assumptions upon which you have based your estimate to be wrong. Where the risk seems very high, then you might try to introduce new activities specifically designed to reduce the risk, or to formulate a contingency action if the risk should materialize. For example, there is not much you can do to stop people getting the flu at a critical time in the project, but you might be able to have a plan to bring in temporary cover for sickness in the case of time-critical activities.

Identify and Quantify Risks for Activities

Look at the assumptions in the plan, such as:

- time required
- availability of staff/resources
- these generate uncertainty
- simple way to handle
- create a most likely estimate for time/effort
- create a second estimate with a safety margin such that the target has a 95% chance of met
- look at the damage that could be caused by a risk
- pick out the most important ones

Plan risk reduction and contingency measures

- risk reduction: activity to stop risk occurring
- contingency: action if risk does occur

Adjust overall plans and estimates to take account of risks

e.g. add new activities which reduce risks associated with other activities

e.g. training, pilot trials, information gathering.

Allocate Resources

Identify and allocate resources to activities. What type of staff is needed for activity? who is (provisionally) available when required You need to allocate resources (staff) to the activities in the plan. Where there is a resource.constraint, that is there are not enough staff (or other resource) of the right type to start all the activities that run in parallel at the planned time, then the start of some activities may need to be delayed until the appropriate resources are available. We have the basic information needed to produce a plan. One way of presenting the plan is by means of a Gantt chart (named after Henry Gantt).

Step 8: Review/Publicize Plan

It is not feasible to produce a detailed plan for all stages of the project right at the beginning of the project planning process and not all the information needed for the detailed planning of the later stages is available at the outset. Initially an outline plan for the whole project would be produced, plus a detailed plan for the first stage.

Review Quality Aspects of the Project Plan

Undertaking one activity can reveal that an earlier activity was not properly completed:

- will have to be reworked
- will require effort and resources
- can lead to loss of control of project
- need to be sure that a completed task is truly completed
- need quality criteria for each task
- tick off when complete
- the list from step 1.1 will help form these document plans and obtain agreement
- Make sure everyone understands and agrees
- Specify this task in a communications plan if need be (as mentioned in step 1.5)

Execute Plan/Lower Levels of Planning

During the project draw up plans for activities in greater detail as they become due. Detail has to wait as more information becomes available. Especially if you are using an iterative development approach. It maintain provisional plans for more important later tasks. Its planning in great detail too soon could be a waste of time.

UNIT SUMMARY

Software Project Management (SPM) is essential for effectively planning, executing, and controlling software development projects. It involves various activities, including defining project scope, managing stakeholders, and ensuring quality. Different plans, methods, and methodologies, such as Agile and Waterfall, are used to structure projects based on their size, complexity, and risk. Project evaluation and programme management help in assessing feasibility, benefits, and risks, while project portfolio management ensures alignment with business goals. Cost-benefit evaluation techniques like ROI and NPV assist in financial decision-making, and risk evaluation helps identify and mitigate potential challenges. Effective programme management ensures optimal resource allocation across multiple projects. An overview of project planning provides insights into scheduling, execution, and monitoring, ensuring successful project delivery.

EXERCISE

1. Explain the concept of project portfolio management and its significance.
2. Discuss the different cost-benefit evaluation techniques used in software project management.
3. How does risk evaluation impact the success of a software project? Provide examples.
4. Describe the role of programme management in handling multiple projects.
5. What are the essential components of an effective project plan?
6. Suppose a company is planning to develop a new e-commerce platform. What factors should be considered in evaluating the project's feasibility?
7. Imagine you are managing a software project with limited resources. How would you allocate resources efficiently?
8. A software development team faces frequent delays due to unclear project scope. How can project planning help mitigate this issue?
9. Consider a scenario where a company is working on multiple software projects simultaneously. How can project portfolio management be applied?
10. A project team encounters unexpected security risks during development. What risk evaluation strategies should they implement?

UUU

UNIT 2

Selection of Appropriate Project Approach, Effort Estimation

RATIONALE

Selecting the right project approach is crucial for successful software development. This unit explores methodologies, process models, and estimation techniques to balance structure and speed of delivery. Accurate effort estimation prevents project delays and budget overruns, ensuring optimal resource allocation. Understanding estimation methods like bottom-up, top-down, parametric models, and COCOMO helps in making informed cost predictions. Additionally, the impact of staffing patterns and schedule compression on project success is examined. Mastering these concepts enables professionals to choose suitable methodologies, estimate costs effectively, and manage project timelines efficiently.

OUTCOMES

- Understand different project approaches and their applicability.
- Identify suitable software methodologies and technologies.
- Analyze software process models and their selection criteria.
- Evaluate software effort estimation techniques and challenges.
- Apply bottom-up, top-down, and parametric estimation models.
- Understand the COCOMO model and cost estimation strategies.
- Assess the impact of staffing patterns and schedule compression on project success.

2.1 SELECTION OF AN APPROPRIATE PROJECT APPROACH

Selecting an appropriate project approach is essential for ensuring the success of a software project. The choice depends on factors such as project complexity, requirement stability, budget constraints, and team expertise. Traditional approaches like Waterfall follow a linear and sequential process, making them suitable for projects with well-defined requirements and minimal expected changes. In contrast, Agile methodologies emphasize iterative development and continuous feedback, making them ideal for projects with evolving requirements. Hybrid approaches combine elements of both, offering flexibility while maintaining structure. The Spiral model focuses on risk assessment through multiple refinement cycles, while the V-Model emphasizes verification and validation at each stage, making it suitable for high-quality control projects. Additionally, the DevOps approach integrates development and operations, supporting continuous integration and deployment. The selection of a project approach is influenced by factors such as project size, time constraints, budget considerations, risk levels, and the expertise of the development team. Choosing the right methodology ensures efficient resource utilization, improved project control, and successful software delivery.

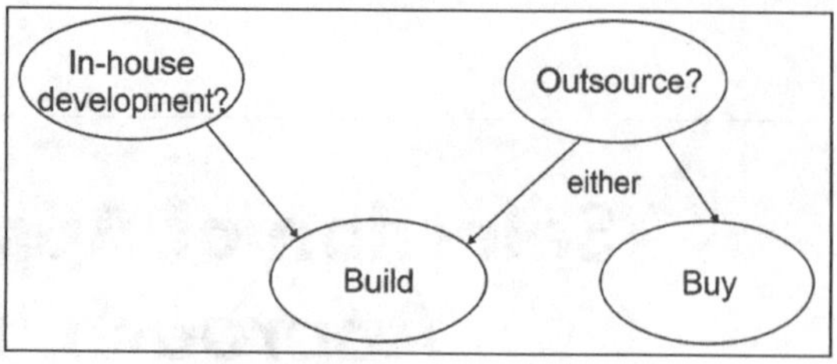

Figure 2.1.

If you were to ask someone to produce, for example, the analysis report in the usability testing scenario, then you would need to explain exactly what you mean by that. This is done via a Product Description. PDs can be re-used from one project to another. A product and the description are relevant to all instances of that product. A specification describes an instance within the class of products. Here we follow the PRINCE approach of firstly identifying the products to be created. These products could be deliverables that will be handed over to the customer or intermediate products such as specifications and design documents that are produced along the way. Selection of projects must take account of possible effects on other projects in the portfolio (example: competition of resource) and the overall portfolio profile (example: specialization versus diversification). In-house development is most of these issues resolved by IS planning and standards. Software houses is more applicable as different customers have different needs and Selection of approach governed by uncertainties of the project properties of application to be built.

2.2 CHOOSING METHODOLOGIES AND TECHNOLOGIES

The development of software in-house suggests that the project has certain characteristics is the project team and the users belong to the same organization; the project being considered slot into a portfolio of existing computer-based system; the methodologies and technologies to be used are not selected by the project manager, but are dictated by local standards.

Outcome of analysis will be selection of most appropriate methodologies and technologies. **Methodologies** (Unified Software Development Process (USDP), Structured system analysis and design methods (SSADM)) **Technologies** (Environments, Software etc). Identify project as either objective driven or product driven and analyses Project Characteristics Data driven or Process driven and general tool or application specific tools available (Graphics etc.) Hardware and software environment and Entertaining games or servicing. Identify project as either objectives-driven or product-driven and analyses other project characteristics.

- Identify High Level Project Risk
- Product uncertainty
- Process uncertainty
- Resource uncertainty
- Take into account user requirements concerning implementation

Methods often involve the creation of models. A model is a representation of a system which certain features but ignores others. For example, an entity relationship diagram (ERD) is an model of the structure of the data used by a system. What can be confusing is that a software development life cycle itself is a type of system. Project analysis should select the most appropriate methodologies and technologies fora project. Methodologies include approaches like the Unified Software Development Process (USDP), Structured Systems Analysis and Design Method (SSADM) and Human-Centred Design, while technologies might include appropriate application-building and automated testing environments. The analysis identifies the methodology, but also selects the methods within the methodology that are to be deployed.

Identify Project as Either Objective-Diven or Product-Driven

The project manager's dream is to have well-defined objectives but as much freedom as possible about how those objectives are to be satisfied. An objective might be to pay staff in a start-up company reliably, accurately and with low administrative costs. The company does not have to specify the use of a particular packaged software solution at the outset — but as we will see, there can be exceptions to this. Sometimes the objectives of the project are uncertain or are the subject of disagreement. People might be experiencing problems, but no one knows exactly how to solve these problems. ICT specialists might provide help with some problems but assistance from other specialists might be needed with others.

Analyze other project characteristics are the following questions can be usefully asked.

Is data-oriented or process-oriented system to be implemented? Data-oriented systems generally mean information systems that will have a substantial database. Process-oriented systems refer to embedded control systems, Ibis not uncommon to have systems with elements of both. Some writers suggest that the approach is more suitable for process-oriented systems Where control is important than for systems dominated by a relational database. Will the software that is to be produced be a general tool or application specific? Are there specific tools available for implementing the particular type of application? Does it involve concurrent processing? Will the system to be created be knowledge based? Will the system to be produced make heavy use of computer graphics? Is the system to be created safety critical? Is the system designed primarily to carry out predefined services or to be engaging and entertaining? What is the nature of the hardware/software environment in which the system will operate?

Identify High Level Project Risk

The greater the uncertainties at the beginning, the greater the risk that the project will be unsuccessful. Once recognize an area of a risk then we can reduce it. Risk is associated with products, processes or resources of a project.

1. Product uncertainty – requirement understanding, environment change, user confusion, government rules.
2. Process uncertainty – extreme programming.
3. Resource uncertainty – availability of staff and other resources.

2.3 SOFTWARE PROCESSES AND PROCESS MODELS

Software product development process usually starts win when request for the product is received from customer for a generic product the marketing department of the company is usually considered customer this expression need for the product is called product inception. From the inception product undergoes is cities of transformations through identifiable stages until it is fully developed released to the customer. After release, the product is used by customer Ann during this time speech. When the product is no longer useful for customer, it is retired. This set of identity able stages in which a project product transit from inception to retirement from the life cycle of the product full stop the software cycle is also commonly their effort to add software development life cycle and software process full stop paragraph a life cycle graphical or textual at the present.

- **Choose the right approach to a project:** variously called technical planning, project analysis, methods engineering and methods tailoring.

- **In-house:** the methods to be used dictated by organizational standards. In-house development almost always involves developing new code. If it is decided to use a specialist organization to implement system, the supplier could either build a bespoke' system for you, or could install a pre- existing application. There are hybrids of these options, e.g. to build in-house but use temporary contract staff, or Customized Off-the-Shelf (COTS) where a basic existing core system is modified for your requirements.
- **Suppliers:** need for tailoring as different customers have different needs. Different types of project need different types of approach. If you are working in one environment which specializes in one type of software, then the approach is likely not to change much from one project to another. Where you work for different clients in different organizations developing a variety of applications then the approach for each project may need to be tailored.

2.4 CHOICE OF PROCESS MODELS

The word 'process' emphasises the idea of this team system in action; in order to achieve an outcome, the system will have to execute one or more activities: this is its process. This applies the development of computer-based applications. A few Interrelated activities have to be undertaken to create a final product. These activities can be organised in different ways and we can call these process model. The planner selects method and specifies how they are to be applied. Not all parts of a methodology search as USDP or SSADM will be compulsory. Many students' projects have the rather basic failing that at fragments such as Top-level data flow diagram and Philip very logical data structure diagram if this is all the project requires it should be explicitly stated.

2.5 STRUCTURE VERSUS SPEED OF DELIVERY

Some object-oriented specialist might object, we include the object-oriented approach as a structured method, it is not unstructured. structured method consists of sets of steps and rules which, when applied, generate system products such as use case diagram. each of these products is defined. these methods are more time consuming to initiative approaches. The RAD Approach there's not use some elements of structured method in Joint application development Workshop call mom developers and users walk together intensively for 3 to 5 days an identify an ugly fully documented system requirement. Often these workshops are conducted for normal business 2 development environments in clean room. Special conference rooms free from outside interruption suitably furnished with whiteboards another is to communication additives of joint application development believe that these conditions can speed up communication and negotiation that might otherwise take several weeks or months.

Use of joint application development does not mean that the project is not structured. The definition all the scope of the project, the initial research involving the interviewing off key personnel and the creation of preliminary data and process models would need to plan and execute before the joint application development sessions where organised. The results of joint application development sessions could be implemented using conventional methods. Joint application development by Jane Wood and Dennis silver answer in 1995 is a useful introduction to joint application development. The set of identifiable stages transits from inception to retirement form the life cycle of the product. The software life cycle is referred to as Software Development Life Cycle (SDLC) and software process.

- Waterfall model
- V-Process model
- Spiral model
- Incremental Delivery
- Software prototype

1. Waterfall Model

It is known as one-shot or once-through model.

Waterfall Model is a design process that is used in software development. It is a linear sequential model that is most effective when the problem statement is well defined and highly structured and all the requirements are known before the commencement of the project. All the essential activities that comprise the software development process are listed in a sequential manner. Development of software happens from one phase to another through a series of non-overlapping phases. Managers can review project progress to see whether the business case for the project is still valid. This is referred to as the stage gate model.

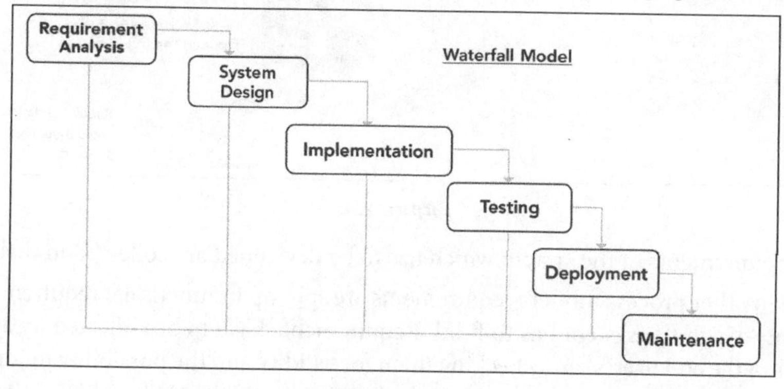

Figure 2.2.

All work on one phase has to be completed and checked off before the next one can start. ISO 12207 is really a technical model showing the order technical processes need to be carried out on a software component. You might break down an application into component increments, but the technical processes relating to that increment are carried out in the ISO 12207 sequence. You can, within the ISO 12207 sequence, loop back in an iterative manner, but the technical sequence still remains.

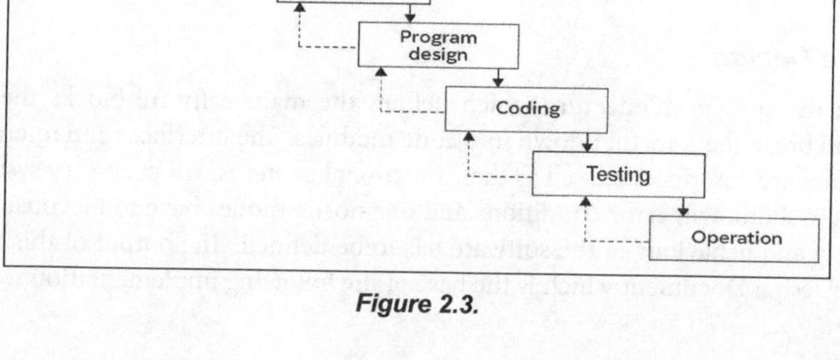

Figure 2.3.

Requirement Analysis & Definition

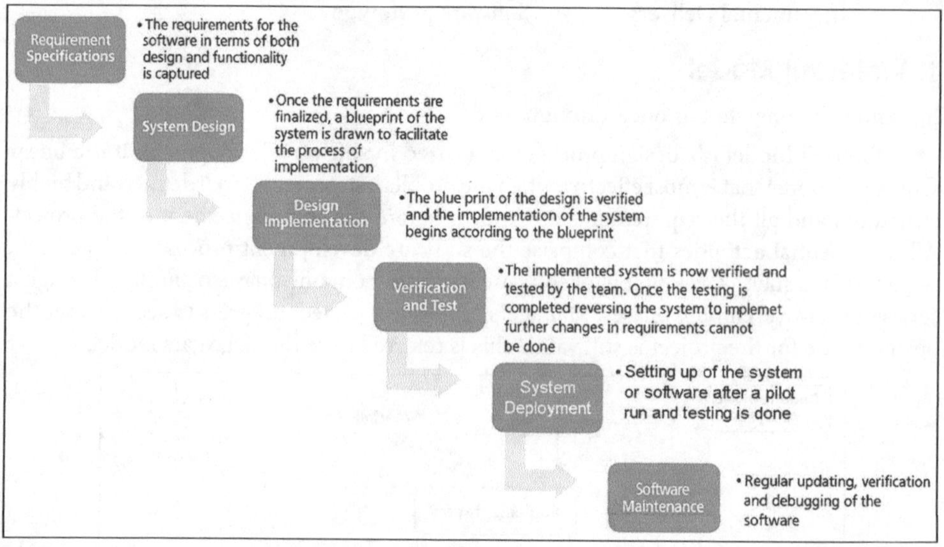

Figure 2.4.

All requirements of the system which has to be developed are collected in this step.

Like in other process model's requirements are split up in functional requirements and constraints which the system has to fulfil. Requirements have to be collected by analyzing the needs of the end user(s) and checking them for validity and the possibility to implement them. The aim is to generate a Requirements Specification Document which is used as an input for the next phase of the model.

System Design

The system has to be properly designed before any implementation is started. This involves an architectural design which defines and describes the main blocks and components of the system, their interfaces and interactions. By this the needed hardware is defined and the software is split up in its components'. this involves the definition or selection of a computer platform, an operating system, other peripheral hardware, etc. The software components have to be defined to meet the end user requirements and to meet the need of possible scalability of the system. The aim of this phase is to generate a System Architecture Document this serves as input for the software design phase of the development, but as an input for hardware design or selection activities. In this phase various documents are generated, one for each discipline, so that the software will receive a software architecture document.

Software Design

Based on the system architecture which defines the main software blocks the software design will break them further down into code modules. The interfaces and interactions of the modules are described, as well as their functional contents. All necessary system states like startup, shutdown, error conditions and diagnostic modes have to be considered and the activity and behaviour of the software has to be defined. The output of this phase is a Software Design Document which is the base of the following implementation work.

Coding

Based on the software design document the work is aiming to set up the defined modules or units and actual coding is started. The system is first developed in smaller portions called units. They are able to stand alone from a functional aspect and are integrated later on to form the complete software package.

Software Integration & Verification

Each unit is developed independently and can be tested for its functionality. This is the so-called Unit Testing. It verifies if the modules or units to check if they meet their specifications. This involves functional tests at the interfaces of the modules, but detailed tests which consider the inner structure of the software modules. During integration the units which are developed and tested for their functionalities are brought together. The modules are integrated into a complete system and tested to check if all modules cooperate as expected. After successfully integration including the related tests the complete system has to be tested against its initial requirements. This will include the original hardware and environment, whereas the previous integration and testing phase may still be performed in a different environment or on a test bench.

Operation & Maintenance

The system is handed over to the customer and will be used the first time by him. The customer will check if his requirements were implemented as expected but he will validate if the correct requirements have been set up in the beginning. In case there are changes necessary it has to be fixed to make the system usable or to make it comply with the customer wishes. In most of the "Waterfall Model" descriptions this phase is extended to a never ending phase of "Operations & Maintenance". All the problems which did not arise during the previous phases will be solved in this last phase.

The Weakness of the Waterfall Model

It is very important to gather all possible requirements during the first phase of requirements collection and analysis. If not all requirements are obtained at once the subsequent phases will suffer from it. Reality is that only a part of the requirements is known at the beginning and a certain percentage will be gathered during the complete development time. Iterations are only meant to happen within the same phase or at best from the start of the subsequent phase back to the previous phase. If the process is kept according to the school book this tends to shift the solution of problems into later phases which results in a bad system design. Instead of solving the root causes the tendency is to patch problems with inadequate measures. There may be a very big "Maintenance" phase at the end. The process only allows for a single run through the waterfall. This could be only a first sample phase which means that the further development is squeezed into the last never ending maintenance phase and virtually run without a proper process.

2. V Process Model

V - Model is an extension of the waterfall model and is based on association of a testing phase for each corresponding development stage. This means that for every single phase in the development cycle there is a directly associated testing phase. This is a highly disciplined model and next phase starts only after completion of the previous phase.

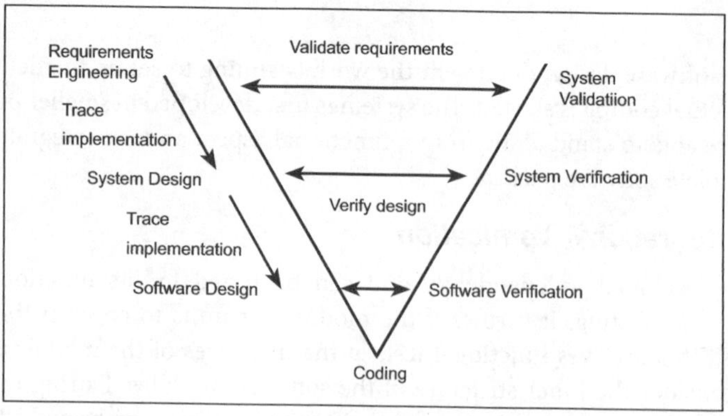

Figure 2.5.

3. Spiral Model

Extends waterfall model by adding iteration to explore/manage risk. Project risk is a moving target. Each loop of the spiral is divided into four quadrants, indicating four stages in each phase. In the first stage of a phase, one or features of the product are analyzed. Those features are identified and resolved through prototyping. In the third stage identified features are implemented using waterfall model. In the fourth and final stage, the developed increment is reviewed by the customer.

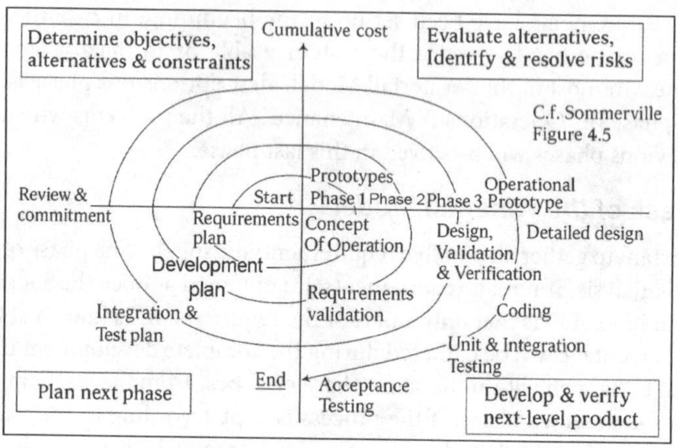

Figure 2.6.

In 1988 Boehm developed the spiral model as an iterative model which includes risk analysis and risk management. On each iteration, identify and solve the sub-problems with the highest risk.

Advantages

1. **Realism:** the model accurately reflects the iterative nature of software development on projects with unclear requirements
2. **Flexible:** incorporates the advantages of the waterfall and evolutionary methods
3. Comprehensive model decreases risk
4. Good project visibility.

Disadvantages

1. Needs technical expertise in risk analysis and risk management to work well.
2. Model is poorly understood by nontechnical management, not so widely used
3. Complicated model needs competent professional management. High administrative overhead.

4. Software Prototyping

This is one way in which we can buy knowledge and reduce uncertainty. A prototype is a working model one or more aspects of the project system. It is constructed and tested quickly and inexpensively in order to test out assumptions.

Evolutionary Delivery: Prototyping

An iterative process of creating quickly and inexpensively live and working models to test out requirements and assumptions Main types: throw away prototypes and evolutionary prototypes. What is prototyped?

- human-computer interface
- functionality

A prototype is a working model of one or aspects of the project application. It is constructed quickly and inexpensively in order to test out assumptions. Learning by doing - useful where requirements are partially known improved communication - users are reluctant to read massive documents, but when system is live you get a better feeling for it improved user involvement user ideas and requests are quickly implemented the reduction of maintenance costs the idea is that if you do not have a prototype then the first release of the application will effectively become a prototype as users will find things that they do not like and then ask for them to be changed. It is easier and safer to make such changes before the application becomes operational. Testing involves devising test cases and then documenting the results expected when the test cases are run. If these are done by hand, then effectively you have a manual prototype.

Incremental Delivery

The incremental build model is a method of software development where the product is designed, implemented and tested incrementally until the product is finished. It involves both development and maintenance. The product is defined as finished when it satisfies all of its requirements. This model combines the elements of the waterfall model with the iterative philosophy of prototyping.

The product is decomposed into a number of components, each of which is designed and built separately. Each component is delivered to the client when it is complete. This allows partial utilization of the product and avoids a long development time. It avoids a large initial capital outlay and subsequent long waiting period. This model of development helps ease the traumatic effect of introducing a completely new system all at once. The incremental model applies the waterfall model incrementally. The series of releases is referred to as increments, with each increment providing functionality to the customers. After the first increment, a core product is delivered, which can already be used by the customer. Based on customer feedback, a plan is developed for the next increments, and modifications are made accordingly. This process continues, with increments delivered until the complete product is delivered. The incremental philosophy is used in the agile process model.

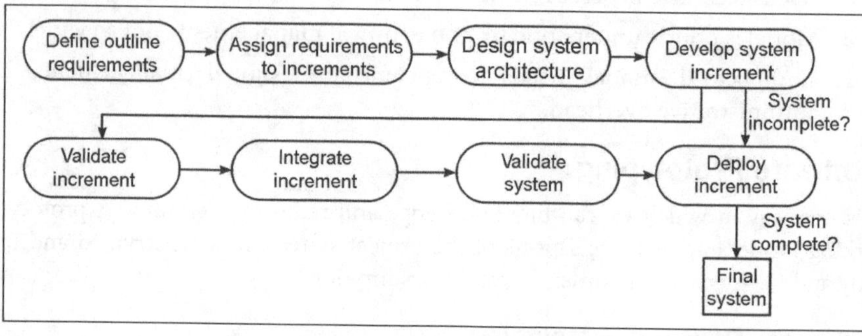

Figure 2.7.

The Incremental model can be applied to DevOps. In DevOps, it centers on the idea of minimizing risk and cost of a DevOps adoption whilst building the necessary in-house skillset and momentum. The application to be delivered is broken down into a number of components each of which will be used by the users. Each of these is then developed as a separate mini- projector increment. Gilb argues that the initial focus should be on high level business objectives. There may be many ways in which important objectives can be achieved and we ought to allow ourselves freedom in the way we try to achieve the objectives.

- **Open technology plan:** we need to ensure that the technologies we use are ones that facilitate the addition of components to an existing application.
- **Plan increments:** the nature and order of the increments to be delivered needs to be delivered to the users have to be planned at the outset.

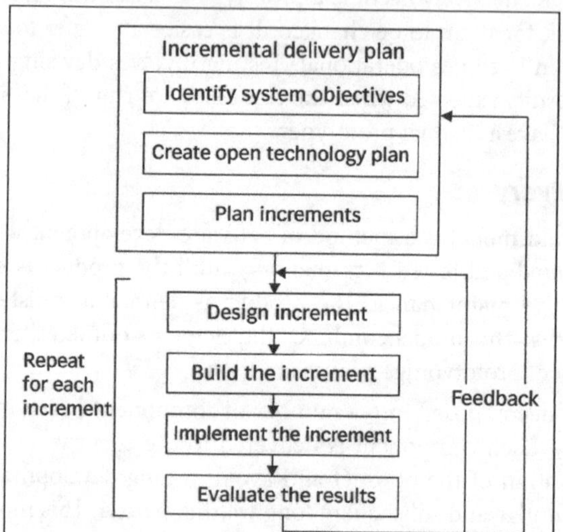

Figure 2.8.

2.6 SOFTWARE EFFORT ESTIMATION

A successful project is one delivered 'on time' within budget and with the required quality'. This implies that targets are set which the project manager then tries to meet. This assumes that the targets are reasonable – no account is taken of the possibility of project manager achieving records levels of productivity from their teams, but still not meeting a deadline because of incorrect initial estimates. Realistic estimates are therefore crucial.

Where are the Estimates Done?

Estimates are carried out at various stages of a software project for a variety of reasons.

- **Strategic planning:** Project portfolio management involves estimating the costs and benefits of new applications in order to allocate priorities. Such estimates may also influence the scale of development staff recruitment.
- **Feasibility study:** This confirms that the benefits of the potential system will justify the costs. System specification: Most system development methodologies usefully distinguish between the definition of the user's requirements and the design which shows how those requirements are to be fulfilled. The effort needed to implement different design proposals will need to be estimated. Estimates at the design stage will also confirm that the feasibility study is still valid. Evaluation of supplier's proposals: In the case of the IOE annual maintenance contracts subsystem.
- **Project Planning:** As the planning and implementation of the project becomes more detailed, more estimates of smaller work components will be made. These will confirm earlier broad-brush estimates and will support more detailed planning, especially staff allocations.

2.7 PROBLEMS WITH OVER AND UNDER-ESTIMATES

The answer to the problem of over-optimistic estimates might seem to be to pad out all estimates, but this itself can lead to problems. You might miss out to the competition who could underbid you, if you were tendering for work. Generous estimates also tend to lead to reductions in productivity. On the other hand, having aggressive targets in order to increase productivity could lead to poorer product quality. Parkinson's law: 'Work expands to fill the time available' that is, given an easy target staff will work less hard. Brooks Law: The effort of implementing a project will go up disproportionately with the number of staff assigned to the project. As the project team grows in size, so will the effort that has to go into management, coordination and communication. This has given rise, in extreme cases to the notion of Brooks Law: putting more people on a late job makes it later'. If there is an over estimate of the effort required, this could lead to more staff being allocated than needed and managerial overheads being increased. Weinberg's Zeroth Law of reliability: 'a software project that does not have to meet a reliability requirement can meet any other requirement'. Most estimating methods need information about past projects. However, care is needed when applying past performance to new projects because of possible differences in factors such as programming languages and the experience of staff. If past project data is lacking, externally maintained datasets of project performance data can be accessed. One well-known international database is that maintained by the International Software Benchmarking Standards Group (ISBSG). which currently contains data from 4800 projects.

Measure of Efforts

Man-month (MM) also referred to as Person-month (PM) is a popular unit fir effort measurement. It quantifies the effort that can be put one person over 1 month. Person-month

(PM) is an appropriate unit for measuring effort as compared to person-day or person-year because developers are assigned project for a certain number of months. Mythical Man-Month "Cost varies as product of men and months, progress does not." Hence the man-month as a unit for measuring the size of job is a dangerous / deceptive myth. The myth of additional manpower Brooks Law: Adding manpower to a late project makes it later.

Mythical Man-Month

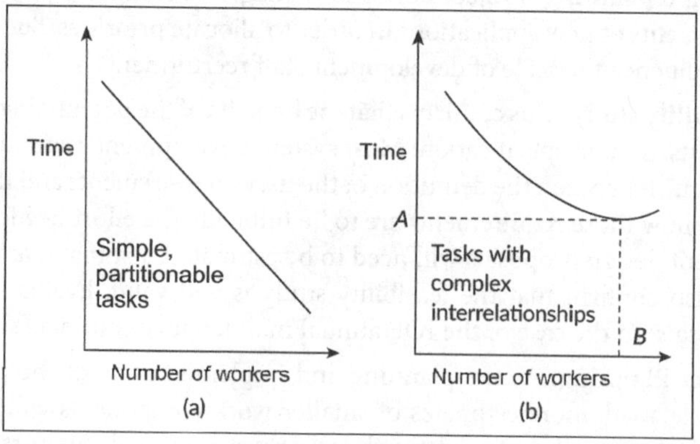

Figure 2.9.

2.8 SOFTWARE EFFORT ESTIMATION TECHNIQUES

Barry Boehm, in his classic work on software effort models, identified the main ways of deriving estimates of software development effort as:

1. Algorithmic models, which use 'effort drivers' representing characteristics of the target system and the implementation environment to predict effort
2. Expert judgement, based on the advice of knowledgeable staff.
3. Analogy, where a similar, completed, project is identified, and its actual effort is used as the basis of the estimate.
4. Parkinson, where the staff effort available to do a project becomes the 'estimate'
5. Price to win, where the 'estimate' is a figure that seems sufficiently low to win a contract.
6. Top-down, where an overall estimate for the whole project is broken down into the effort required for component tasks.
7. Bottom-up, where component tasks are identified and sized and these individual estimates are aggregated.

Whereas 'Parinkson' method is not really an effort prediction method, but a method of setting the scope of a project. Similarly, 'price to win' is a way of identifying a price and not a prediction. Therefore, Boehm rejects these two methods. So, there are five methods to study the software effort estimation.

2.9 BOTTOM-UP ESTIMATION, TOP-DOWN APPROACH AND PARAMETRIC MODELS

With the bottom-up approach the estimator breaks the project into its component tasks. With a large project, the process of breaking it down into tasks is iterative: each task is decomposed into its component subtasks and these in turn could be further analyzed. It is suggested that this is repeated until you get tasks an individual could do in a week or two. The bottom-up part comes in adding up the calculated effort for each activity to get an overall estimate. The bottom-up approach is best at the later, more detailed, stages of project planning. If this method is used earlier, assumptions about the characteristics of the final system and project work methods will have to be made. Where a project is completely novel or there is no historical data available, the estimator would be forced to use the bottom-up approach.

Bottom-up estimating steps:

1. Break project into smaller and smaller components .
2. Stop when you get to what one person can do in one/two weeks.]
3. Estimate costs for the lowest level activities.
4. At each higher level calculate estimate by adding estimates for lower levels

A procedural code-oriented approach The bottom-up approach described above works at the level of activities. In software development a major activity is writing code. Here we describe how a bottom-up approach can be used at the level of software components.

1. Envisage the number and type of software modules in the final system.
2. Estimate the SLOC of each identified module.
3. Estimate the work content, taking into account complexity and technical difficulty.
4. Calculate the work-days effort.

Historical data can be used to provide ratios to convert weighted SLOC to effort. Note that the above Steps can be used to derive an estimate of lines of code that can be used as an input to one of the COCOMO models which are described later.

The Top-down Approach and Parametric Models

The top-down approach is normally associated with parametric (or algorithmic) models. These may be explained using the analogy of estimating the cost of rebuilding a house. Analogy/Example: Unless the house-owner is in the building trade he or she is unlikely to be able to calculate the numbers of bricklayer-hours, carpenter-hours, electrician-hours, and so on, required. Insurance companies, however, produce convenient tables where the house-owner can find estimates of rebuilding costs based on such parameters as the number of storeys and the floor space of a house. This is a simple parametric model. Project effort relates mainly to variables associated with characteristics of the final system. A parametric model will normally have one or more formulae in the form:

effort = (system size) X (productivity rate).

For example, system size might be in the form 'thousands of lines of code' (KLOC) and have the specific value of 3 KLOC while the productivity rate was 40 days per KLOC. These values will often be matters of judgement. A model to forecast software development effort therefore has two key components. The first is a method of assessing the amount of the work needed. The second assesses the rate of work at which the task can be done. For example, Amanda at IOE may estimate that the first software module to be constructed is 2 KLOC. She may then judge that if Kate undertook the development of the code, with her expertise she could work at a rate of 40 days per KLOC per day and complete the work in 2 × 40 days, i.c. 80 days, while Ken, who is Jess experienced, would need 55 days per KLOC and take 2 × 55, i.e. 110 days to complete the task. In this case KLOC is a size driver indicating the amount of work to be done, while developer experience is a productivity driver influencing the productivity or work rate. If you have figures for the effort expended on past projects (in work-days for instance) and also the system sizes in KLOC, you should be able to work out a productivity rate as productivity = effort/size A more sophisticated way of doing this would be by using the statistical technique least squares regression to derive an equation in the form:

effort = constant, + (size × constant)

Some parametric models, such as that implied by function points, are focused on system or task size, while others, such are COCOMO, are more concerned with productivity factors.

Top-down Estimates Steps

Produce overall estimate using effort driver(s), distribute proportions of overall estimate to components. Bottom-up is use when no past project data identify all tasks that have to be done so quite time-consuming use when you have no data about similar past projects Top-down is produce overall estimate based on project cost drivers is based on past project data divide overall estimate between jobs to be done.

Parametric Models

Some models focus on task or system size e.g. Function Points. FPs originally used to estimate Lines of Code, rather than effort.

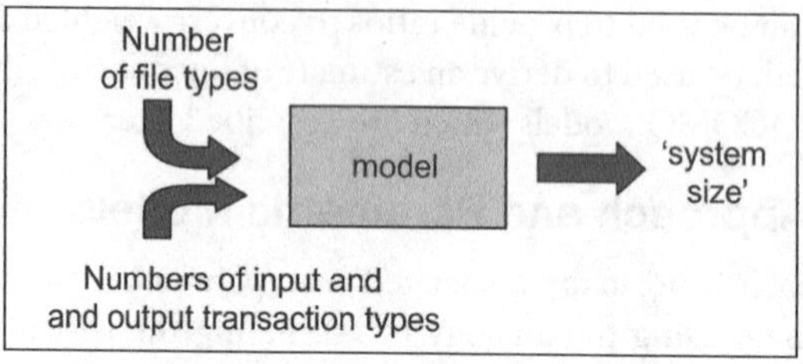

Figure 2.10.

'System size' here can be seen as an index that allows the size of different applications to be compared. It will usually correlate to the number of lines of code required.

Parametric models - the need for historical data simplistic model for an estimate

estimated effort = (system size) / productivity

Example: system size = lines of code

productivity = lines of code per day

productivity = (system size) / effort

based on past projects

Other models focus on productivity: e.g. COCOMO Lines of code (or FPs etc.) an input

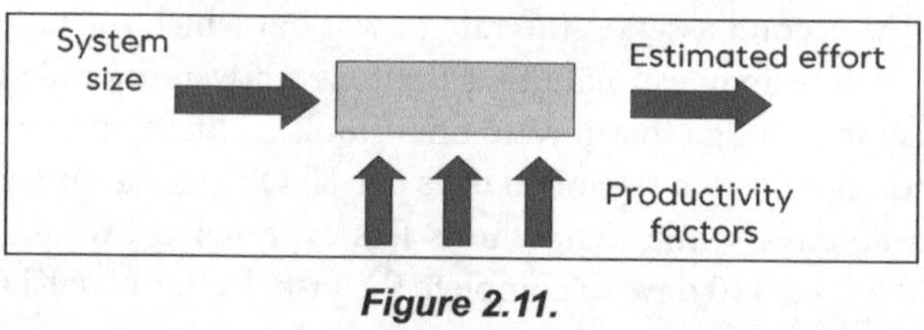

Figure 2.11.

COCOMO (lines of code) and function points are the examples of these problem with COCOMO. COCOMO originally was based on a size parameter of lines of code (actually 'thousands of delivered source code instructions' or kdsi). Newer versions recognize the use of functions points as a size measure, but convert them to a number called equivalent lines of code (eloc).

Function points model system size, while COCOMO focuses on productivity factors.

1. Albrecht/ the International FP User Group (IFPUG) function points
2. Symons/Mark II function points
3. COSMIC function points
4. COCOMO81 and COCOMO II

1. Albrecht/IFPUG Function Points

Albrecht worked at IBM and needed a way of measuring the relative productivity of different programming languages. Needed some way of measuring the size of an application without counting lines of code. Identified five types of components or functionality in an information system. Counted occurrences of each type of functionality in order to get an indication of the size of an information system.

Different programming languages have different degrees of power' which relate to the ratio between the length of programming commands and the amount of processing they create. This is analogous to trying to assess the productivity of bricklayers where different bricklayers work with bricks of different sizes. One way of dealing with this problem is to say that what is important is the size of the wall being built not the number of bricks it contains. FPs are way of measuring the amount of functionality in an application without counting the lines of code in the application.

Five function types of Albrecht function points

1. **Logical Interface File (LIF) types:** equates roughly to a datastore in systems analysis terms. Created and accessed by the target system
2. **External Interface File (EIF) types:** where data is retrieved from a datastore which is actually maintained by a different application.
3. **External Input (EI) types:** input transactions which update internal computer files
4. **External Output (EO) types:** transactions which extract and display data from internal computer files. Generally, involves creating reports.
5. **External Enquiry (EQ) types:** user-initiated transactions which provide information but do not update computer files. The user inputs some data that guides the system to the information the user needs.

External user types	Low complexity	Medium complexity	High complexity
EI	3	4	6
EO	4	5	7
EQ	3	4	6
LIF	7	10	15
EIF	5	7	10

The complexity of each instance of each user type is assessed and a rating applied. Originally this assessment was largely intuitive, but later versions, developed by IFPUG have rules governing how complexity is rated.

Examples:

Payroll application has:

1. Transaction to input, amend and delete employee details – an EI that is rated of medium complexity
2. A transaction that calculates pay details from timesheet data that is input – an EI of high complexity
3. A transaction of medium complexity that prints out pay-to-date details for each employee – EO
4. A file of payroll details for each employee – assessed as of medium complexity LIF

A personnel file maintained by another system is accessed for name and address details – a simple EIF.

FP counts:

1. Medium EI	4 FPs
2. High complexity EI	6 FPs
3. Medium complexity EO	5 FPs
4. Medium complexity LIF	10 FPs
5. Simple EIF	5 FPs
Total	30 FPs

If previous projects delivered 5 FPs a day, implementing the above should take 30/5 = 6 days.

Function points Mark II:

Builds on work by Albrecht and a simpler method.

Work originally for CCTA:

Should be compatible with SSADM; mainly used in UK. It has developed in parallel to IFPUG FPs. Mark II FPs is a version of function points developed in the UK and is used by a minority of FP specialists. Mark II version has simpler rules and thus provides an easier introduction to the principles of FPs. The IFPUG rules are best to consult IFPUG documentation.

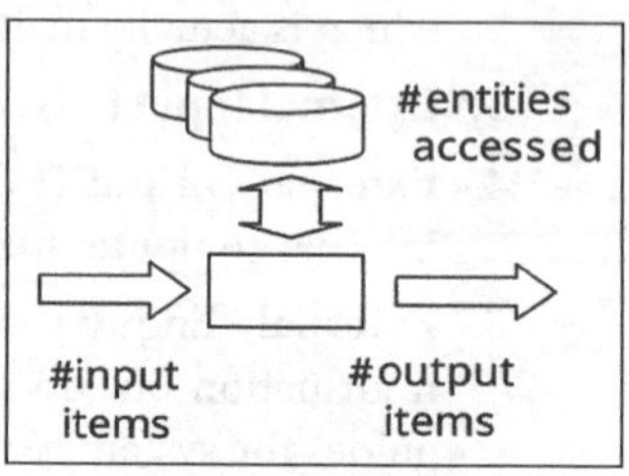

Figure 2.12.

FP count = $N_i * 0.58 + N_e * 1.66 + N_o * 0.26$

For each transaction (cf use case) count the number of input *types* (not occurrences e.g. where a table of payments is input on a screen so the account number is repeated a number of times), the number of output types, and the number of entities accessed. Multiply by the weightings shown and sum. This produces an FP count for the transaction which will not be very useful.

Sum the counts for all the transactions in an application and the resulting index value is a reasonable indicator of the amount of processing carried out. The number can be used as a measure of size rather than lines of code.

Function points for embedded systems:

- Mark II function points, IFPUG function points were designed for information systems environments
- COSMIC FPs attempt to extend concept to embedded systems
- Embedded software seen as being in a particular layer in the system
- Communicates with other layers and also other components at same level

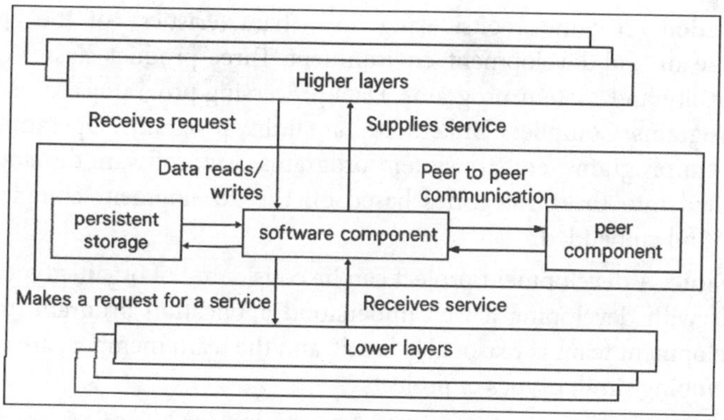

***Figure 2.13.** Layered software*

Attempts have been made to extend IFPUG FPs to real-time and embedded systems, but this has not been very convincing (IMHO). Embedded software component is seen as at a particular level in the system. It receives calls for services from a higher layer and requests services from lower layers. It will receive responses from lower levels and will send responses to higher levels.

2.10 COCOMO MODEL, COST ESTIMATION

The problems with COCOMO are that the input parameter for system size is an estimate of lines of code. This is going to have to be an estimate at the beginning of the project. Function points, as will be seen, counts various features of the logical design of an information system and produced an index number which reflects the amount of information processing it will have to carry out. This can be crudely equated to the amount of code it will need.

Problem with COCOMO

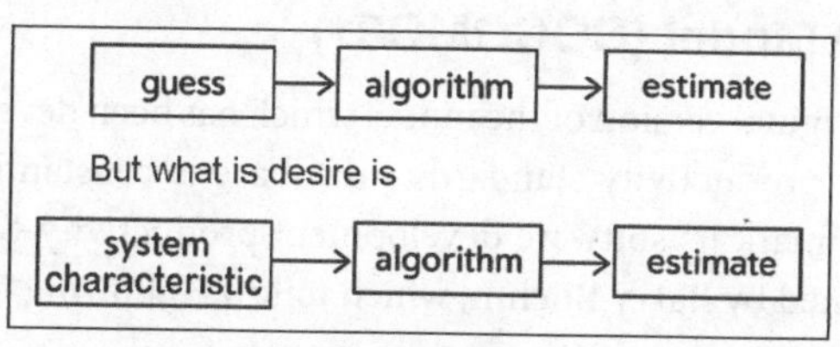

Figure 2.14.

COCOMO (COnstructive COst estimation MOdel) was proposed by Barry Boehm is the most popular method which is categorized in algorithmic methods. This method uses some equations and parameters, which have been derived from previous experiences about software projects for estimation. The models have been widely accepted in practice. Code-size S is given in thousand (Kilo) LOC (KLOC) and Effort is in person-month. The input parameter for system size is an estimate of lines of code. This is going to have to be an estimate at the beginning of the project. Function points count various features of the logical design of an information system and produced an index number which reflects the amount of information processing it will have to carry out. This can be crudely equated to the amount of code it will need.

Classification of COCOMO

The classification is done considering the characteristics of the product, the development team and development environment. Three product classes correspond to application, utility and system programs. Data processing programs are considered to be application programs. Compilers, linkers, etc., are utility programs. Operating systems and real-time system programs, etc. are system programs. Any software development project can be classified into three categories based on the development complexity: organic, semidetached and embedded.

- **Organic:** A development project can be considered of organic type, if the project deals with developing a well understood application program, the size of the development team is reasonably small, and the team members are experienced in developing similar types of projects.
- **Semidetached:** A development project can be considered of semidetached type, if the development consists of a mixture of experienced and inexperienced staff. Team members may have limited experience on related systems but may be unfamiliar with some aspects of the system developed.
- **Embedded:** A development project is considered to be of embedded type, if the software developed is strongly coupled to complex hardware, or if the stringent regulations on the operational procedures exist.

Basic Model

$$\text{effort} = c \times \text{size } k$$

c and k depend on the type of system: organic, semi-detached, embedded Size is measured in kloc i.e., Thousands of lines of code.

According to Boehm, software cost estimation should be done through three stages: Basic COCOMO, Intermediate COCOMO, and Complete COCOMO.

Basic COCOMO Model (COCOMO81)

COCOMO81 is the original version of the model which has been developed into COCOMO II. Based on industry productivity standards - database is constantly updated. Allows an organization to benchmark its software development productivity. Simple COCOMO was the first model suggested by Barry Boehm, which follows following formula:

$$\text{Effort} = a^*(\text{KLOC})b,$$

where S is the code-size, and a, b are complexity factors which depend on the type of system: organic, semi-detached, embedded. This model use three sets of a, b depending on the complexity of the software. COCOMO model is simple and easy to use.

The basic COCOMO model gives an approximate estimate of the project parameters. The basic COCOMO estimation model is given by the following expressions:

Effort = a * (KLOC)b PM Tdev = 2.5 * (Effort)c Months

Where, KLOC is the estimated size of the software product expressed in Kilo Lines of Code a, b, c are constants for each category of software products. Tdev is the estimated time to develop the software, expressed in months. Effort is the total effort required to develop the software product, expressed in Person Months (PMs) the effort estimation is expressed in units of PM. The value of the COCOMO constants a, b, c are given in the following table:

Software project	a	b	c
Organic	2.4	1.05	0.38
Semi-detached	3.0	1.12	0.35
Embedded	3.6	1.20	0.32

Intermediate COCOMO Model

In the intermediate COCOMO, nominal effort estimation is obtained using the power function with three sets of a, b, with coefficient a slightly different from that of the basic COCOMO.

Model	a	b
Organic (Simple in terms of size and complexity)	3.2	1.05
Semiditched (Average in terms of size and complexity)	3.0	1.15
Embedded (Complex)	2.8	1.20

The basic COCOMO model assumes that effort and development time are functions of the product size alone. Many other project parameters apart from the product size affect the development effort and time required for the product. In order to obtain an accurate estimation of the effort and project duration, the effect of all relevant parameters must be taken into account. The intermediate COCOMO model recognizes this fact and refines the initial estimate obtained using the basic COCOMO expressions by using a set of 15 cost drivers (multipliers) based on various attributes of software development.

Complete COCOMO Model

Both the basic and intermediate COCOMO models consider a software product as a single homogeneous entity. Most large systems are made up several smaller sub-systems, each of them in turn could be of organic type, some semidetached, or embedded. The complete COCOMO model takes into account these differences in characteristics of the subsystems and estimates the effort and development time as the sum of the estimates for the individual subsystems. This approach reduces the percentage of error in the final estimate.

The following development project can be considered as an example application of the complete COCOMO model. A distributed Management Information System (MIS) product for an organization having offices at several places across the country can have the following following sub-components:

- Database part
- Graphical User Interface (GUI) part
- Communication part

Of these, the communication part can be considered as embedded software. The database part could be semi-detached software, and the GUI part organic software. The costs for these three components can be estimated separately, and summed up to give the overall cost of the system. COCOMO (lines of code) and function point are the examples of Algorithmic/Parametric models.

COCOMO II A Parametric Productivity Mode

An updated version of COCOMO: There are different COCOMO II models for estimating at the early design stage and the post architecture stage when the final system is implemented. The core model:

$$pm = A(size)(sf) \times (em1) \times (em2) \times (em3)....$$

where pm = person months, A is 2.94, size is number of thousands of lines of code, sf is the scale factor, and em is an effort multiplier.

For example, if modern programming practices are used, the initial estimates are scaled downward by multiplication with a cost driver having a value less than 1. Each of the 15 attributes receives a rating on a six-point scale that ranges from "very low" to "extra high". An effort multiplier from the table below applies to the rating. The product of all effort multipliers results in an Effort Adjustment Factor (EAF).

EAF is used to refine the estimates obtained by basic COCOMO as follows:

Effort|corrected = Effort * EAF

Tdev|corrected = 2.5 * (Effort|corrected) c

Based on five factors which appear to be sensitive to system size.

1. PRECedentedness (PREC). Degree to which there are past examples that can be consulted.
2. Development FLEXibility (FLEX). Degree of flexibility that exists when implementing the project
3. Architecture/risk RESoLution(RESL). Degree of uncertainty about requirements
4. TEAM cohesion (TEAM).
5. Process MATurity (PMAT) could be assessed by Capability Maturity Model Integration (CMMI).

Cost Drivers	**Ratings**					
	Very Low	**Low**	**Nominal**	**High**	**Very High**	**Extra High**
Product attributes						
Required software reliability	0.75	0.88	1.00	1.15	1.40	
Size of application database		0.94	1.00	1.08	1.16	
Complexity of the product	0.70	0.85	1.00	1.15	1.30	1.65

Cost Drivers	Ratings					
	Very Low	Low	Nominal	High	Very High	Extra High
Hardware attributes						
Run-time performance constraints			1.00	1.11	1.30	1.66
Memory constraints			1.00	1.06	1.21	1.56
Volatility of the virtual machine environment		0.87	1.00	1.15	1.30	
Required turnabout time		0.87	1.00	1.07	1.15	
Personnel attributes						
Analyst capability	1.46	1.19	1.00	0.86	0.71	
Applications experience	1.29	1.13	1.00	0.91	0.82	
Software engineer capability	1.42	1.17	1.00	0.86	0.70	
Virtual machine experience	1.21	1.10	1.00	0.90		
Programming language Experience	1.14	1.07	1.00	0.95		
Project attributes						
Application of software engineering met hods	1.24	1.10	1.00	0.91	0.82	
Use of software tools	1.24	1.10	1.00	0.91	0.83	
Required development schedule	1.23	1.08	1.00	1.04	1.10	

An example of use of the table is as follows.

Driver	Very low	Low	Nominal	High	Very high	Extra high
PREC	6.20	4.96	3.72	2.48	1.24	0.00
FLEX	5.07	4.05	3.04	2.03	1.01	0.00
RESL	7.07	5.65	4.24	2.83	1.41	0.00
TEAM	5.48	4.38	3.29	2.19	1.10	0.00
PMAT	7.80	6.24	4.68	3.12	1.56	0.00

A software development team is developing an application which is very similar to previous ones it has developed. A very precise software engineering document lays down very strict requirements. PREC is very high (score 1.24). FLEX is very low (score 5.07). The good news is that these tight requirements are unlikely to change (RESL is high with a score 2.83). The team is tightly knit (TEAM has high score of 2.19), but processes are informal (so PMAT is low and scores 6.24).

The formula for sf is

sf = B + 0.01 × Σ scale factor values

i.e. sf = 0.91 + 0.01× (1.24 + 5.07 + 2.83 + 2.19 + 6.24) = 1.0857

If system contained 10 kloc then estimate would be 2.94 × 101.0857 = 35.8 person month. Using exponentiation (to the power of) adds disproportionately to the estimates for larger applications.

2.11 STAFFING PATTERN AND EFFECT OF SCHEDULE COMPRESSION

Resource allocation in software development is important and many methods have been proposed. This introduces the staffing pattern as a metric of resource distribution among project phases, and verifies its effect on software quality and productivity using real project data.

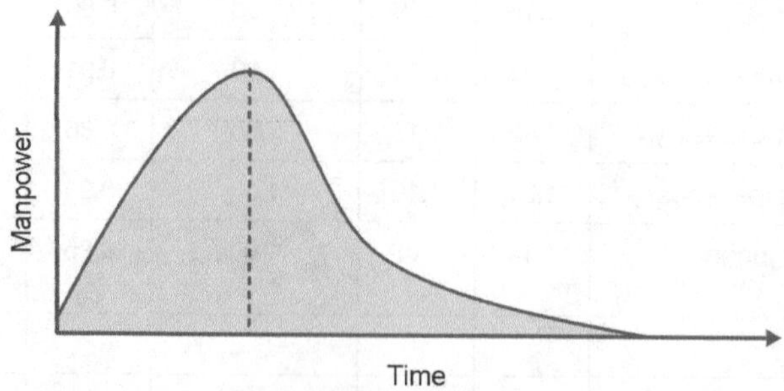

Figure 2.15.

The main findings are there exist different staffing patterns in reality; the staffing pattern has significant effect on software quality (post- release defect density); the staffing pattern has no significant effect on productivity; the effort invested on test, document or code inspection possibly explains the effect of staffing pattern on software quality; the effort consumed by rework counteracts the effect of other potential factors on productivity. Preliminary heuristics are suggested to resource allocation practices. Norden was one of the first to investigate staffing pattern. Considered general Research and Development (R&D) type of projects.

Norden concluded:

Staffing pattern for any R&D project can be approximated by the lay leigh distribution curve.

Putnam adapted the Rayleigh-Norden curve:

Related the number of delivered lines of code to the effort and the time required to develop the product.

Studied The Effect of Schedule Compression

Example

If the estimated development time using COCOMO formulas is 1 year:

Then to develop the product in 6 months, the total effort required (and the project cost) increases 16 times.

Boehm's Result

There is a limit beyond which a software project cannot reduce its schedule by buying any personnel or equipment. This limit occurs roughly at 75% of the nominal time estimate for small and medium sized projects

Capers Jones' Estimating Rules of Thumb

Empirical Rules

Formulated based on observations No scientific basis Because of their simplicity,These rules are handy to use for making off-hand estimates. Give an insight into many aspects of a project for which no formal methodologies exist yet.

Capers Jones' Rules

Rule 1: SLOC-function point equivalence:

One function point = 125 SLOC for C programs.

Rule 2: Project duration estimation:

Function points raised to the power 4 predicts the approximate development time in calendar months.

Rule 3: Rate of requirements creep:

User requirements creep in at an average rate of 2% per month from the design through coding phases.

Rule 4: Defect removal efficiency:

Each software review, inspection, or test step will find and remove 30% of the bugs that are present.

Rule 5: Project manpower estimation:

The size of the software (in function points) divided by 150 predicts the approximate number of personnel required for developing the application.

Rule 6: Number of personnel for maintenance

Function points divided by 500 predicts the approximate number of personnel required for regular maintenance activities.

Rule 7: Software development effort estimation:

The approximate number of staff months of effort required to develop a software is given by the software development time multiplied with the number of personnel required.

Staffing patterns as follows:

1. **Rapid-team-buildup pattern:**

   The staffing levels peak in requirement phase, and decrease in later phases. This might mean the culture of excessive documentation or design, leading to low ability to respond rapidly for requirement change. Another possible reason would be to outsource part of the system to other organization for design and development. In both situations, we suppose the software quality and productivity are low.

2. **Fix-staff pattern:**

   The team size is fixed or stable across project lifecycle. It is likely that the same team has done all work. Due to sufficient learning time and communication within the team, we assumed that high software quality will be yielded as a result. It is hard to assess its productivity: peoples work efficiently due to effective communication; this effect cannot counteract against the excessive human resources investment in a prolonged duration.

UNIT SUMMARY

This unit explores the selection of an appropriate project approach, methodologies, and estimation techniques to ensure effective software development and project management. Choosing the right project approach, such as Waterfall, Agile, Hybrid, or DevOps, depends on factors like project complexity, requirement stability, and team expertise. Similarly, selecting suitable software development methodologies and technologies, including frameworks, programming languages, and cloud platforms, is crucial for project success. Various software process models, such as Waterfall, Agile, Spiral, and RAD, provide structured development approaches, and choosing the right model depends on factors like project size, risk, and flexibility requirements. A key challenge in software development is balancing structure and speed of delivery, ensuring quality while meeting time-sensitive demands. Software effort estimation plays a vital role in predicting the time, resources, and costs required for project completion. However, inaccurate estimates, whether over or under, can lead to budget overruns, missed deadlines, and resource mismanagement. Different estimation techniques, including expert judgment, analogy-based estimation, and algorithmic models, help improve accuracy. Additionally, approaches like bottom-up estimation, which starts at the task level, and the top-down approach, which considers the overall project scope, provide different perspectives on effort estimation. Parametric models and the COCOMO (Constructive Cost Model) technique further assist in predicting project costs and resource requirements. Lastly, factors like staffing patterns and schedule compression impact project timelines, influencing overall efficiency and success.

EXERCISES

1. How do Agile and Waterfall methodologies differ in software development?
2. Explain the difference between structured development and rapid delivery in software projects.
3. Why is software effort estimation important in project management?
4. What is the purpose of parametric models in software effort estimation?
5. Describe the COCOMO model and its role in cost estimation.
6. Explain the significance of balancing structure and speed of delivery in software projects.
7. How do staffing patterns impact project success? Provide examples.
8. A company is developing a mobile application with rapidly changing requirements. Which project approach and process model would you recommend, and why?
9. A software development team is working on a large-scale project and needs to estimate effort and cost. How can they use the COCOMO model for estimation?
10. A manager wants to speed up project delivery by compressing the schedule. What potential risks and challenges might arise, and how can they be managed?

UUU

UNIT 3

Activity Planning And Risk Management

RATIONALE

Effective software project management requires careful activity planning, scheduling, and risk management. This unit explores techniques for sequencing activities, network planning models, and resource allocation strategies. Understanding risk identification, assessment, and mitigation ensures project stability and success. Critical path creation and cost estimation help optimize project timelines and budget management. By mastering these concepts, professionals can enhance efficiency, minimize uncertainties, and ensure the smooth execution of software projects. Proper resource scheduling and allocation further contribute to meeting project goals within constraints.

OUTCOMES

- Understand activity planning and project scheduling techniques.
- Learn sequencing methods and network planning models.
- Identify, assess, and manage project risks effectively.
- Develop strategies for risk mitigation and countermeasures.
- Optimize resource allocation and scheduling processes.
- Create critical paths and analyze cost implications.

3.1 ACTIVITY PLANNING

Feasibility Assessment

Is the project possible within required timescales and resource constraints? It is not until we have constructed a detailed plan that we can forecast a completion date with any reasonable knowledge of its achievability.

Resource Allocation

What are the most effective ways of allocating resources to the project? When should the resources be available? The project plan allows us to investigate the relationship between timescales and resource availability.

Detailed Costing

How much will the project cost and when is that expenditure likely to take place? After producing an activity plan and allocating specific resources, we can obtain detailed estimates of costs and their timing.

Motivation

Providing targets and seen to monitor achievement against targets is an effective way of motivating staff, where they have been involved in setting those targets in the first place.

Co-ordination

When does the staff in different departments need to be available to work on a project and when does staff need to be transferred between projects? The project plan, with large projects involving than a single project team, provides an effective vehicle for communication and coordination among teams.

Activity planning and scheduling techniques place an emphasis on completing the project in a minimum time at an acceptable cost or, alternatively, meeting a set target date at minimum cost. One effective way of shortening project durations is to carry out activities in parallel.

Scheduling

Time is nature's way of stopping everything happening at once. Having worked out a method of doing the project identified the tasks to be carried assessed the time needed to do each task need to allocate dates/times for the start and end of each activity.

3.2 PROJECT SCHEDULES AND PROJECTS AND ACTIVITIES

A stage of a larger project, the project plan must be developed to the level of showing dates when each activity should start and finish and when and how much of each resource will be required. Once the plan has been refined to this level of detail we call it a project schedule. Creating a project schedule comprises four stages.

The first step in producing the plan is to decide what activities need to be carried out and in what order they are to be done_ From this we can construct an ideal activity plan that is, a plan of when each activity would ideally be undertaken were resources not a constraint.

Second step the ideal activity plan will then be the subject of an activity risk analysis, aimed at identifying potential problems. This might suggest alterations to the ideal activity plan and will almost certainly have implications for resource allocation. Third step is resource allocation. The expected availability of resources might place constraints on when certain activities can be carried out, and our ideal plan might need to be adapted to take account of this resource allocation. The final step is schedule production. Once resources have been allocated to each activity, we will be in a position to draw up and publish a project schedule which indicates planned start and completion dates.

ACTIVITIES

Activity networks help us to assess the feasibility of the planned project completion date to identify when resources will need to be deployed to activities and calculate when costs will be incurred. This helps the co-ordination and motivation of the project team. Activity networks are based on some assumptions:

- A project is composed of a number of activities
- A project may start when at least one of its activities is ready to start.
- A project will be completed when all of the activities it encompasses have been completed.

Defining Activities

If an activity must have a clearly defined start and a clearly defined end-point, marked by the production of a tangible deliverable. An activity requires a resource then that resource requirement must be forecast able and is assumed to be required at a constant level throughout the duration of the activity. The duration of an activity must be forecastable assuming normal circumstances, and the reasonable availability of resources. Some activities might require that others are completed before they can begin. (Precedence requirements). Where some of these assumptions do not apply (e.g. clearly defined start and end-points, certainty of durations) there are complicated techniques that can be applied, e.g. PERT risk.

Identifying Activities

Approaches to identifying the activities or tasks that make up a project:

- The Activity based approach
- The Product-based approach
- The Hybrid approach

1. The Activity Based Approach

The activity-based approach consists of creating a list of all the activities that the project is thought to involve. This might involve a brainstorming session involving the whole project team or it might stern from an analysis of similar past projects. When listing activities, for a large project, it might be helpful to subdivide the project into the main life-style stages and consider each of these separately. The risks of omitting or double-counting tasks, a much-favored way of generating a task list is to create a Work Breakdown Structure (WBS). Work-based draw-up a WBS listing the work items needed. WBS involves

- identifying the main tasks
- break each main task down into subtasks
- The subtasks can further be broken down into lower-level tasks.

Activities are added to a branch in the structure if they directly contribute to the task immediately above if they do not contribute to the parent task, then they should not be added to that branch. The tasks at each level in any branch should include everything that is required to complete the task at the higher level if they are not a comprehensive definition of the parent task, then something is missing. When preparing a WBS, consideration must be given to the final level of detail.

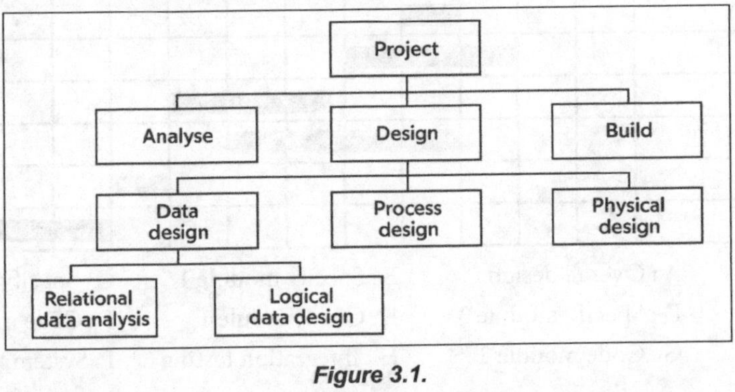

Figure 3.1.

2. Product Based Approach

Activity planning is carried out in Steps 4 and 5 list the deliverable and intermediate products of project Product Breakdown Structure (PBS). Identify the order in which products have to be created work out the activities needed to create the products. PBS show how a system can be broken down into different products for development. Product Flow Diagram (PFD) indicates, for each product, which products are required as inputs?

3. The Hybrid Approach

A mix of the activity-based approach and the product-based approach used approach. WBS consists of a list of the products of the project; and a list of activities for each product.

3.3 SEQUENCING AND SCHEDULING ACTIVITIES

Throughout a project, we will require a schedule that clearly indicates when each of the project's activities is planned to occur and what resources it will need. The chart shown has been drawn up taking account of the nature of the development process that is, certain tasks must be completed before others may start and the resources that are available (for example, activity C follows activity B because Andy cannot work on both tasks at the same time).In drawing up the chart, we have therefore done two things we have sequenced the tasks and scheduled. The scheduling has had to take account of the availability of staff and the ways in which the activities have been allocated to them. The schedule might look different were there a different number of staff or were we to allocate the activities differently. In the case of small projects, this combined sequencing—scheduling approach might be suitable, where we wish to allocate individuals to tasks at an early planning stage.

On larger projects it is better to separate out these two activities: to sequence the tasks according to their logical relationships and then to schedule them taking into account resources and other factors. Approaches to scheduling that achieve this separation between the logical and the physical use networks to model the project. A project plan as a bar chart tells us who is doing what and when. The final outcome of the planning process is as follows:

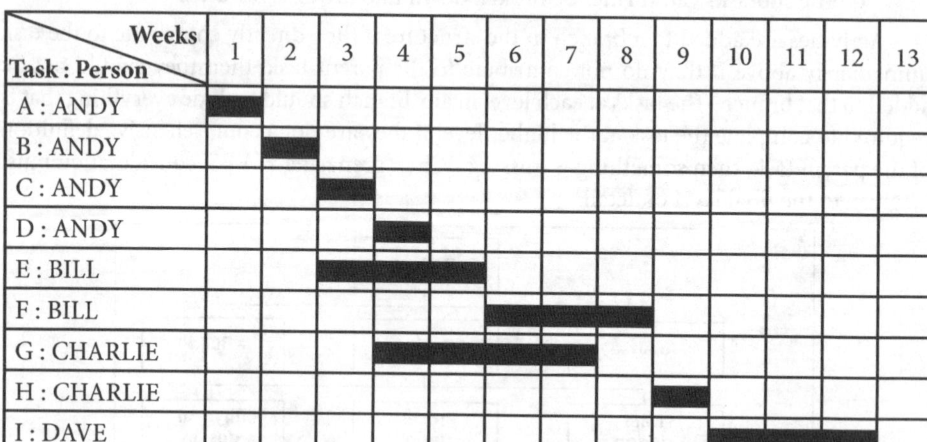

Activity key A : Overall design B : Specify module 1 C : Specify module 2
D : Specify module 3 E : Code module 1 F : Code module 3
G : Code module 2 H : Integration testing I : System testing

3.4 NETWORK PLANNING MODELS

Project Evaluation and Review Technique (PERT) is a project management tool used to schedule, organize, and coordinate tasks within a project. PERT was devised to support the development of the Polaris missile. CPM It was developed by Du Pont Chemical Company.

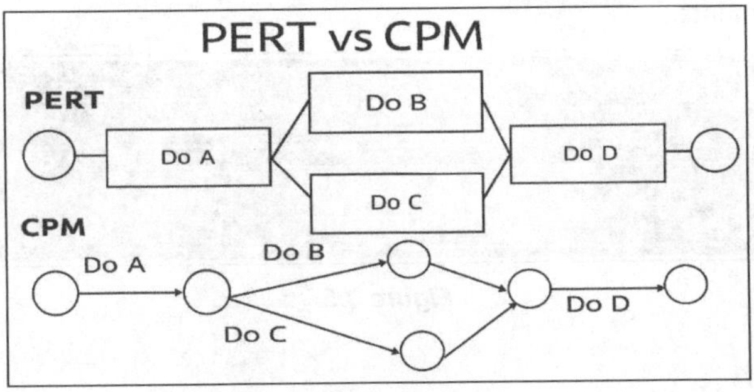

Figure 3.2.

PERT is an activity-on-node notation the nodes 'are the boxes which represent activities. CPM uses an activity-on-arrow notation where the arrows are the activities. The approached described here is based on PERT.

Drawing up a PERT Diagram

No looping back is allowed – deal with iterations by hiding them within single activities

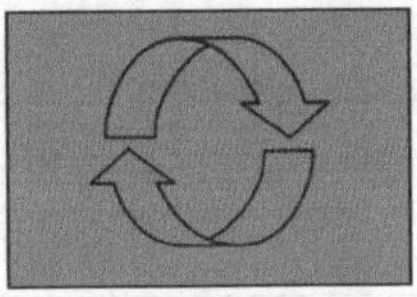

Milestones activities, such as the start and end of the project, which indicate transition points. They have zero duration.

Lagged activities: Where there is a fixed delay between activities e.g. s days' notice has to be given to users that a new release has been signed off and is to be installed.

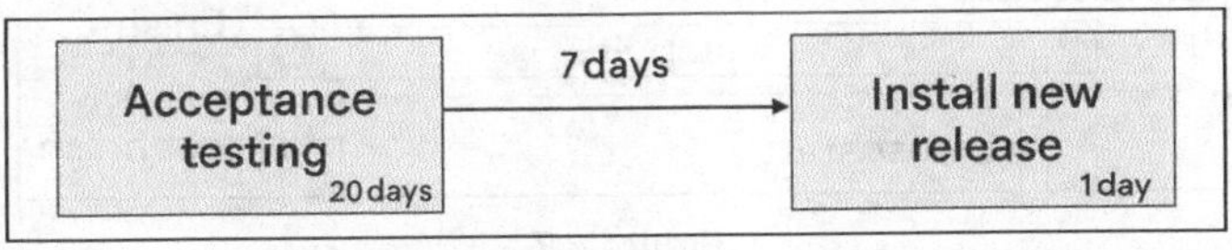

Figure 3.3.

Types of Links Between Activities

Finish to start: The following activity starts when the previous one has been finished. e.g., testing starts when coding has been completed.

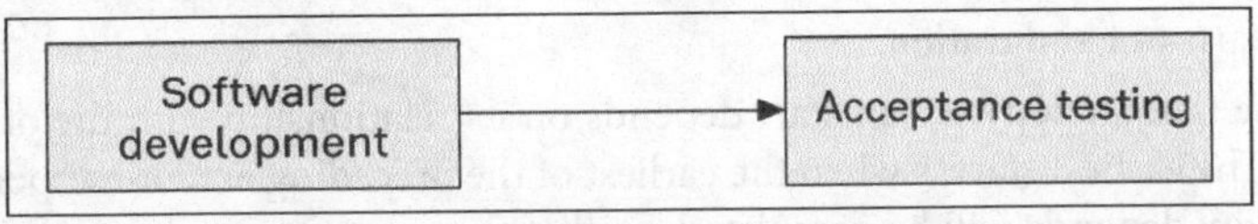

Figure 3.4.

Start to Start/Finish to Finish

- **Start to start:** When one activity starts another has to start as well. e.g. when prototype testing starts amendment documentation has to start as well.
- **Finish to finish:** when one activity finishes the other must finish too. e.g. when the testing of the prototype is completed so is the documentation of any amendments.

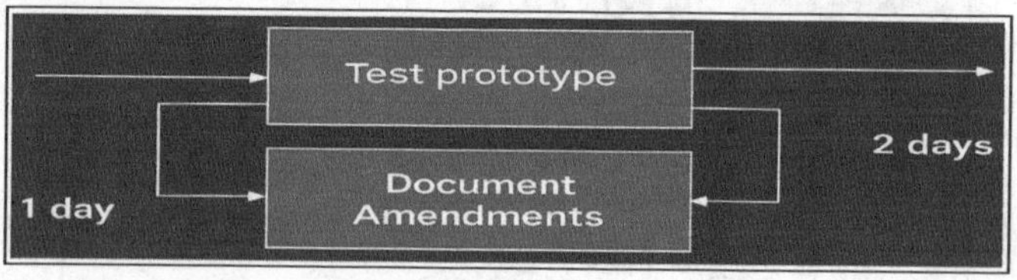

Figure 3.5.

Start to Finish

In the example when the cutover to the new system takes place, the operation of the temporary system is no longer needed. Although the cutover depends of the acceptance testing to be completed, the implication is that the cutover might not start straight after acceptance testing.

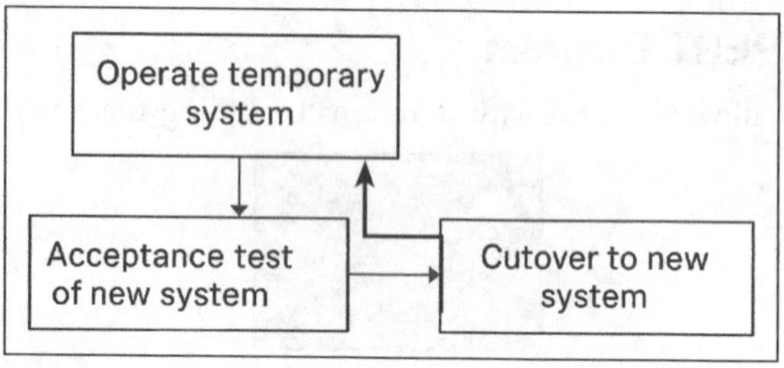

Figure 3.6.

Start and Finish Times

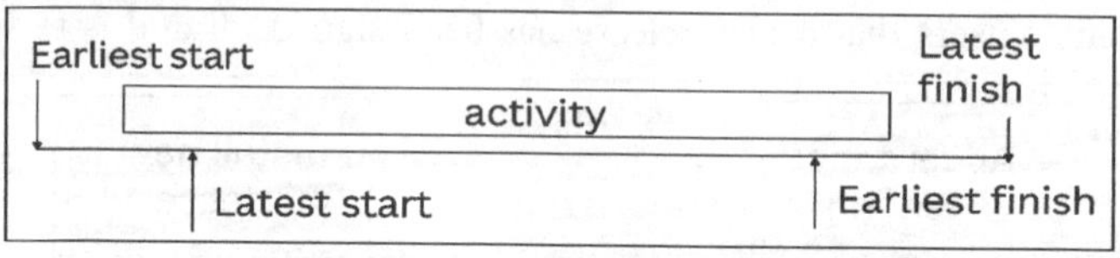

Figure 3.7.

- Activity write report software
- Earliest start (ES)
- Earliest finish (EF) = ES + duration

Latest finish (LF) = latest task can be completed without affecting project end.

Latest start = LF – duration.

The time that an activity can start depends on its relationship with the other tasks in the project. The earliest start is when the earliest of the preceding activities upon which the current activity depends will be completed, so that the current one can start. If it starts at this time the earliest the current activity can finish is the earliest start plus its duration. It may be that the activity, although it can start, can be delayed because later activities do not have to start right way. This gives us a latest finish date. The latest start date is the latest finish date less the duration of the activity.

Example:

Earliest start = day 5 latest finish = day 30 duration = 10 days earliest finish = ?

latest start = ?

Float = LF - ES - duration

What is it in this Case?

The earliest finish (EF) would be day 5 plus 10 days i.e. day 15. The latest start (LS) would be day 30 – 10 days i.e. day 20. The float would be 30 – 5 – 10 = 15 days This is same as LF – EF or LS – ES. Day 0: In the last example, day numbers used rather than actual dates. Makes initial calculations easier – not concerned with week-ends and public holidays. For finish date/times Day 1 means at the END of Day 1. For a start date/time Day 1 means at the END of Day 1.The first activity begins at Day 0 i.e. the end of Day 0 i.e. the start of Day 1.This means activity A could finish on Day 5, for example, and a dependent activity B could then start on Day 5 as well (not Day 6). All this may make sense if you think about activities that finish and start halfway through a day. We talk about Days', other time units could be equally valid e.g. Hours, weeks, months. We assume 5 day working weeks in our calculations – unless otherwise specified. You could use these with lags e.g. documentation of the changes to the prototype starts 1 day after the testing and finishes 2 days after testing has been completed. These project scheduling techniques model the project's activities and their relationships as a network. Both of these techniques used an activity-on-arrow approach to visualizing the project as a network where activities are drawn as arrows joining circles, or nodes, which represent the possible start and or completion of an activity or set of activities.

Formulating a Network Model

The first stage in creating a network model is to represent the activities and their relationships as a graph. In activity-on-node we do this by representing activities as nodes in the graph-the lines between nodes represent dependencies. Constructing precedence networks:

- A project network should have only one start node.
- A project network should have only one end node.
- A node has duration and Links have no duration.
- Precedents are the immediate preceding activities.

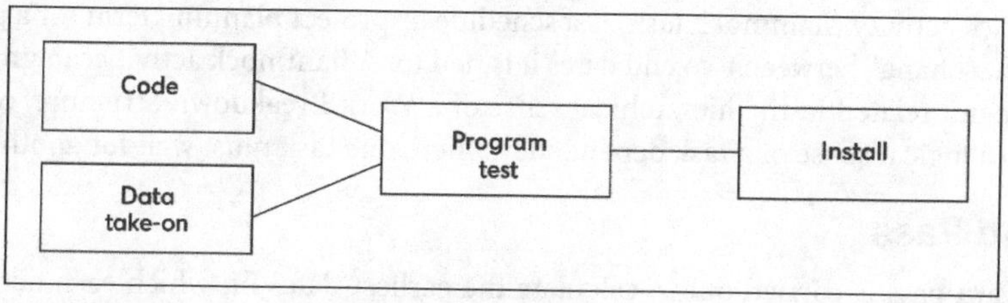

Figure 3.8.

- A network may not contain loops.

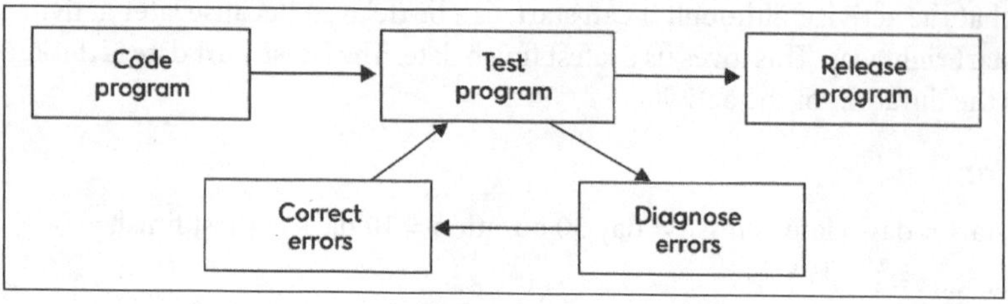

Figure 3.9.

- Times moves from left to right
- A network should not contain dangles.

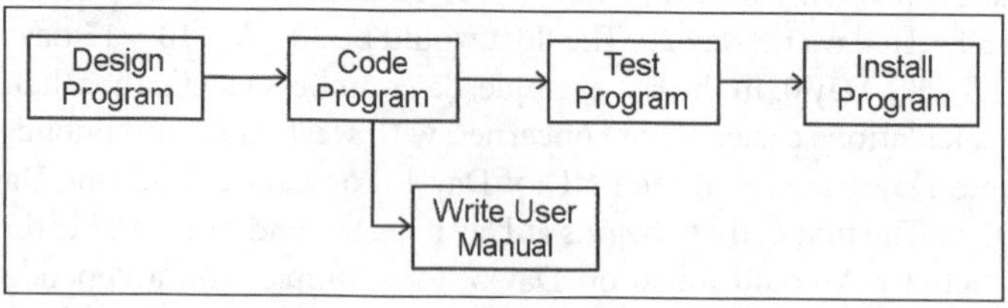

Figure 3.10.

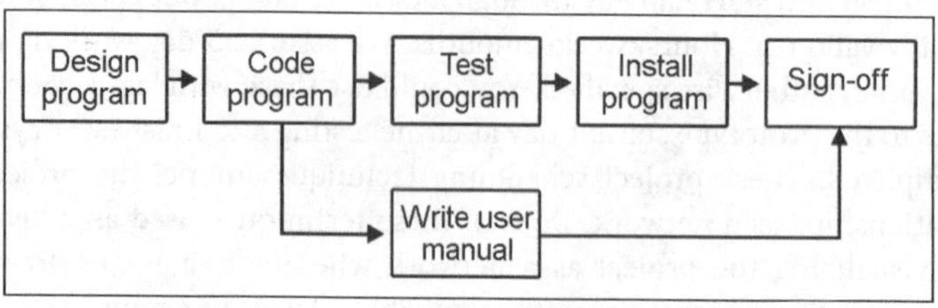

Figure 3.11.

Representing Lagged Activities

We might come across situations where we wished to undertake two activities in parallel so long as there is a lag between the two. We might wish to document amendments to a program as it was tested - if evaluating a prototype. Where activities can occur in parallel with a time lag between them we represent the lag with duration on the linking arrow as shown in Figure. This indicates that documenting amendments can start one day after the start of prototype testing and will be completed two days after prototype testing is completed.

Hammock Activities

A hammock activity (hammock task) is a schedule or project planning term for a grouping of tasks that "hang" between two end dates it is tied to. A hammock activity can group tasks which are not related in the hierarchical sense of a Work Breakdown Structure, or are not related in a logical sense of a task dependency where one task must wait for another.

Forward Pass

The forward pass is carried out to calculate the earliest dates on which each activity may be started and completed.

Start at beginning (Day 0) and work forward following chains. Earliest start date for the current activity = earliest finish date for the previous

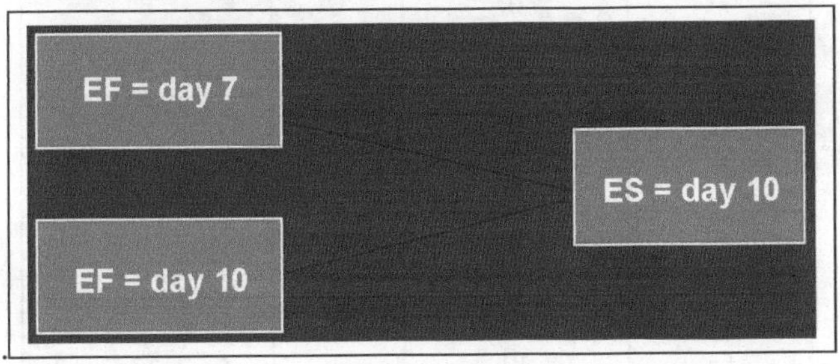

Figure 3.12.

When there is than one previous activity, take the latest earliest finish. The forward pass and the calculation of earliest start dates are calculated according to the following reasoning:

- Activities A, B and F may start immediately, so the earliest date for their start is zero.
- Activity A will take 6 weeks, so the earliest it can finish is week 6.
- Activity B will take 4 weeks, so the earliest it can finish is week 4.
- Activity F will take 10 weeks, so the earliest it can finish is week 10.
- Activity C can start as soon as A has finished so its earliest start date is week 6. It will take 3 weeks so the earliest it can finish is week 9.

Example of an Activity Network

Work out the earliest start and end dates for each activity. Activities D and E can start as soon as B is complete so the earliest they can each start is week 4. Activity D, which will take 4 weeks, can therefore finish by week 8 and activity E, which will take 3 weeks, can therefore finish by week 7.

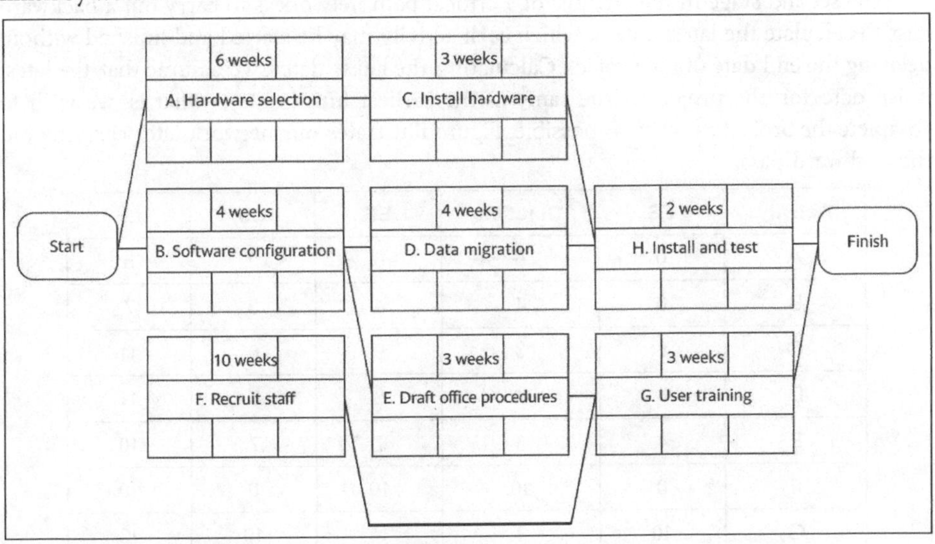

Figure 3.13.

Activity	ES duration	EF	Latest Finish
A	0	6	6
B	0	4	4
C	6	3	9
D	4	4	8
E	4	3	7
F	0	10	10
G	10	3	14
H	9	2	11

Activity G cannot start until both E and F have been completed. It cannot therefore start until week 10 — the later of weeks 7 (for activity E) and 10 (for activity F). It takes 3 weeks and finishes in week 13.Similarly, Activity H cannot start until week 9 — the later of the two earliest finished dates for the preceding activities C and a.The project will be complete when both activities H and G have been completed. The earliest project completion date will be the later of weeks 11 and 13— that is, week 13.

Backward Pass

Start from the *last* activity

Latest Finish (LF) for last activity = Earliest Finish (EF)

work backwards

Latest finish for *current* activity = Latest start for the *following*

than one following activity - take the *earliest* LS

Latest Start (LS) = LF for activity - duration

The second stage in the analysis of a critical path network is to carry out a backward pass to calculate the latest date at which each activity may be started and finished without delaying the end date of the project. Calculating the latest dates, we assume that the latest finish date for the project is the same as the earliest finish date — that is, we wish to complete the project as early as possible. Figure illustrates our network alter carrying out the backward pass.

Activity	ES	Duration	EF	LS	LF
A	0	6	6	2	8
B	0	4	4	3	7
C	6	3	9	8	11
D	4	4	8	7	11
E	4	3	7	7	10
F	0	10	10	0	10
G	10	3	14	10	13
H	9	2	11	11	13

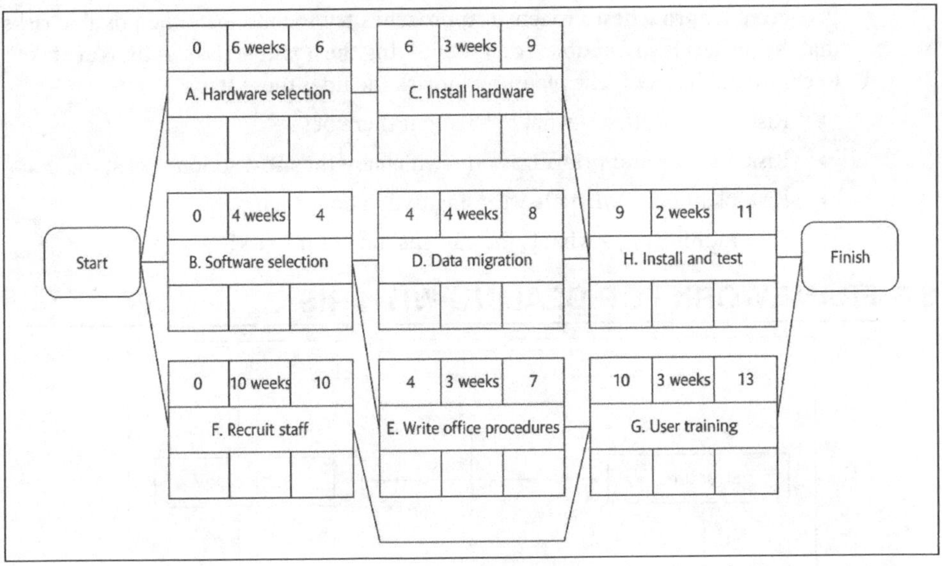

Figure 3.14.

The latest activity dates are calculated as follows. The latest completion date for activities G and 1-1 is assumed to be week 13. Activity H must therefore start at week 11 at the latest (13-2) and the latest start date for activity G is week 10 (13-3). The latest completion date for activities C and D is the latest date at which activity H must start — that is. Week 11. They therefore have latest start dates of week 8 (11-3) and week 7 (11-4) respectively. Activities E and F must be completed by week 10 so their earliest start dates are weeks 7 (10-3) and 0 (10-10 respectively. Activity B must be completed by week 7 the latest start date for both activities D and El so its latest start is week 3 (7-4). Activity A must be completed by week 8 (the latest start date for activity C) so its latest start is week 2 (8-6). The latest start date for the project start is the earliest of the latest start dates for activities A, B and F. This is week zero. If the project does not start on time it won't finish on time.

3.5 RISK MANAGEMENT

Good risk management may identify situations where an unexpected future t might present an opportunity to be exploited e.g. a task less difficult than expected.It process begins when somebody asks what kind of ts can damage the business and how much damage can be done. Identifying and measuring the potential loss exposures, choosing the most efficient methods of controlling and financing loss exposure and implementing them and finally monitoring all the outcomes are the main steps involved in Risk Management.

Risk Management Approaches

Risk Management approaches can broadly be classified into Reactive and Proactive. The latter approach is much effective in risk handling.

- **Reactive Approaches**: Reactive Approaches take no action an unfavorable t occurs. Once an unfavorable t occurs, these approaches try containing the adverse effects associated with the risk and take steps to prevent future occurrence of the same risk events.

- **Proactive Approaches:** Proactive Approaches try to anticipate the possible risks that the project is susceptible. After identifying the possible risks, actions are taken to eliminate the risks. The planning for risk includes these steps:
    - Risk identification – what risks might there be?
    - Risk analysis and prioritization – which are the most serious risks?
    - Risk planning – what are we going to do about them?
    - Risk monitoring – what is the current state of the risk?

3.6 FRAMEWORK FOR DEALING WITH RISK

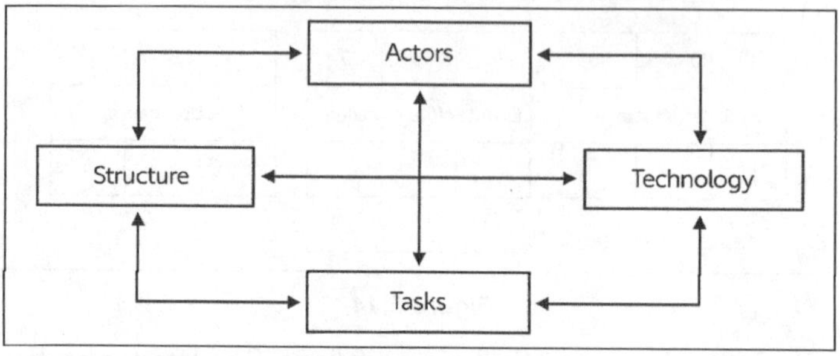

Figure 3.15.

This is based on Lyytinen's sociotechnical model of risk Actors relate to all those involved in the project including both developers, users and managers e.g. a risk could be that high staff turnover leads to information of importance to the project lost

- **Technology**: That used to implement the project and that embedded in the project deliverables risk could be that the technologies selected are not in fact appropriate.
- **Structure:** this includes management procedures, risk here is that a group who need to carry out a project task are not informed of this need because they are not part of the project communication network.
- **Tasks:** the work to be carried out. A typical risk is that the amount of effort needed to carry out the task is underestimated. A risk could be well belonged to than one of the four areas for example, estimates wrong could be influenced by problems with actors (e.g. lack of experience with a technical domain) or the structure (over optimism of managers keen to win work).
- **Technology:** the methods, techniques and tools to be used on various types of risks; Financial risk is the loss of key resources like funding, etc. In this case the company will not have adequate cash flow to meet financial obligations.

Types of Financial Risks

Credit risk, Investment risk, liquidity risk, market risk and operational risks. When the borrower becomes default and was unable to make payments as promised it is said to be Credit risk, called default risk. Investment risk was associated with this where the investor losses his principal and interest too. Due to lack of liquidity in the market an asset cannot be sold to make the profit or to prevent a loss this is what called as Liquidity risk. Due to the change in value of the market risk factors value of investment portfolio or the value of a trading portfolio will decrease. Foreign exchange rates, stock prices, interest rates, and commodity prices are the standard Market risk factors. A risk arising from execution of an organization's business functions is Operational risk. Risks arising from the people, systems and processes through which an organization operates.

Other Categories of Financial Risks

Fraud risks, legal risks, physical or environmental risks. Risky business processes that could lead to project failure are Process risks. Those risks that are associated with damage to the reputation of an organization or its brand are Intangible risks. Risks which involve things connected to time are Time risks. Losses of critical employees or knowledge which are connected to man power are Human risks. include government regulations and the same having an impact on the operations of the company are Legal Risks. Physical risks are those losses of physical resources such as equipment, buildings, land, etc. due to natural disasters or manmade.

3.7 RISK IDENTIFICATION, RISK ASSESSMENT, RISK PLANNING AND RISK MANAGEMENT

Approaches to identifying risks include:

- Use of checklists – based on the experience of past projects.
- Brainstorming – getting knowledgeable stakeholders together to pool concerns.
- Causal mapping – identifying possible chains of cause and effect.
- Boehm's top 10 development risks:

Barry Boehm surveyed software engineering project leaders to find out the main risks that they had experienced with their projects. For each risk, some risk reduction techniques has been suggested.

Risk	Risk reduction techniques
Personnel shortfalls	Staffing with top talent; job matching; teambuilding; training and career development; early scheduling of key personnel
Unrealistic time and cost estimates	Multiple estimation techniques; design to cost; incremental development; recording and analysis of past projects; standardization of methods.
Developing the wrong software functions	Improved software evaluation; formal specification methods; user surveys; prototyping; early user manuals

Gold plating refers to inclusion of features that in fact are unnecessary and which end up never used.

Assessment – Monitoring

Risk Prioritization

Risk Exposure (RE) = (potential damage) × (probability of occurrence)

Ideally Potential damage: a money value e.g. a flood would cause **£0.5** millions of damage. Probability 0.00 (absolutely no chance) to 1.00 (absolutely certain) e.g. 0.01 (one in hundred chance)

RE = **£0.5m** x 0.01 = **£5,000**

Crudely analogous to the amount needed for an insurance premium.If there were 100 people chipping in **£5,000** each, there would be enough for the 1 in 100 chance of the flooding. If there were 2 floods then the system collapses. In practice, with project risks, these quantitative approaches are impractical and qualitative approaches are used instead.

	Hazard	Likelihood	Impact	Risk exposure
R1	Changes to requirements specification during coding	1	8	8
R2	Specification takes longer than expected	3	7	21
R3	Staff sickness affecting critical path activities	5	7	35
R4	Staff sickness affecting non-critical activities	10	3	30
R5	Module coding takes longer than expected	4	5	20
R6	Module testing demonstrates errors or deficiencies in design	1	10	10

Risk Probability: Qualitative Descriptors

Probability level	Range
High	Greater than 50% chance of happening
Significant	30-50% chance of happening
Moderate	10-29% chance of happening
Low	Less than 10% chance of happening

Managers would be happier identifying an approximate range rather than a precise probability. Qualitative descriptors of impact on cost and associated range values

Impact level	Range
High	Greater than 30% above budgeted expenditure
Significant	20 to 29% above budgeted expenditure
Moderate	10 to 19% above budgeted expenditure
Low	Within 10% of budgeted expenditure

Similar tables can be produced for the impact on project duration and on the quality of project deliverables. The problem with the qualitative approach is how do you combine the judgements about probability and impact – you can't multiply them together.

Probability Impact Matrix

R1, R2 etc refer to risks. They are located on the grid according to the likelihood and impact ratings that have been allocated to them. A zone around the top right hand corner of the grid can be designated and risks falling within that zone are treated as requiring urgent action.

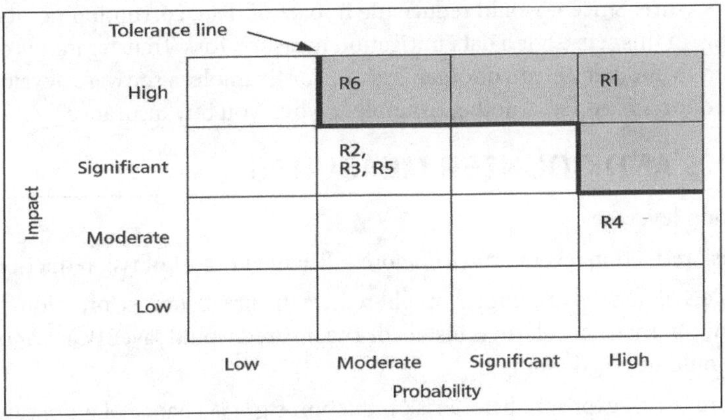

Figure 3.16.

Risk Planning

Risk planning consists of drawing up contingency plans and where appropriate, adding these to the project's task structure. With small projects, risk planning is the responsibility of the project manager, but medium or large projects will benefit from the appointments of a full-time risk manager. Risks can be dealt with by:

- **Risk acceptance:** the cost of avoiding the risk may be greater than the actual cost of the damage that might be inflicted.
- **Rik avoidance:** avoid the environment in which the risk occurs e.g. buying an OTS application would avoid a lot of the risks associated with software development e.g. poor estimates of effort.
- **Risk reduction:** the risk is accepted but actions are taken to reduce its likelihood e.g. prototypes ought to reduce the risk of incorrect requirements.
- **Risk mitigation/contingency measures:** tries to reduce the impact if the risk does occur e.g. taking backups to allow rapid recovery in the case of data corruption.
- **Risk transfer:** the risk is transferred to another person or organization. The risk of incorrect development estimates can be transferred by negotiating a fixed price contract with an outside software supplier.
- **Risk Acceptance:** This is deciding to do nothing about the risk. This means you will accept its consequences. In order to concentrate on the likely or damaging risks, the damage that those risks could cause would be less than the costs needed to act towards reducing their probability of occurrence.
- **Risk Avoidance:** Some activities are so prone to accidents that it is best to avoid them altogether. Example to avoid all the problems associated with developing software solutions from scratch, a solution could be to: Buy an off-the-shelf product.

Risk Reduction attempts to reduce the likelihood of the risk occurring. For example, consider the following risk: developers leaving a company in the middle of a project for a better paid job. In order to reduce the probability of such a risk occurring: the developers could be promised to be paid generous bonuses on successful completion of the project.

Risk Mitigation is the action taken to ensure that the impact of the risk is reduced when it occurs. Taking regular backups of data storage, is it a risk mitigation measure or a risk reduction measure. Since it would reduce the impact of data. corruption not its likelihood of happening, in this sense it is a data mitigation measure. Risk Transfer in this case the risk is transferred to another person or organization. For Example, a software development task is outsourced for a fixed fee. Another example is when you buy insurance.

3.8 RISKS AND COUNTER MEASURES

Risk reduction leverage

Risk reduction leverage = (REbefore – REafter) / (cost of risk reduction)

Example: An insurance company might reduce the fire insurance premium from £2k to £1k on condition that a fire alarm is installed. The insured would save£1k a year by investing £500 so it would be worth doing.

REbefore is risk exposure before risk reduction e.g. 1% chance of a fire causing £200k damage.

REafter is risk exposure after risk reduction e.g. fire alarm costing £500 reduces probability of fire damage to 0.5%.

RRL = (1% of £200k) – (0.5% of £200k)/£500 = 2.

RRL > 1.00 therefore worth doing.

Probability Chart

An estimate of activity duration is realistically a range of values clustered around the most likely value that are trailing off on either side of this central value. How can we take account of this in project planning? PERT risk technique

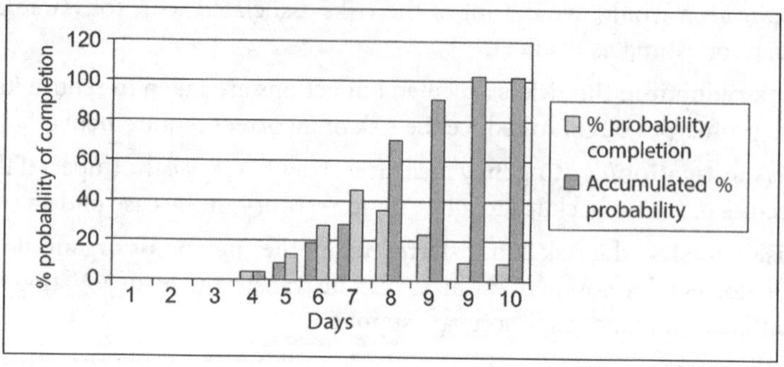

Figure 3.17.

PERT Technique

Project Evaluation and Review Technique (PERT) is a project management tool used to schedule, organize, and coordinate tasks within a project. PERT is used to evaluate the effects of uncertainty. It estimation considers three values:

- Optimistic estimate (O) – the shortest time that could be realistically be expected
- Most likely estimate (M) - the time we would expect the task to take .
- Pessimistic estimate (Least likely estimate (L)) - worst possible time (only 1% chance of worse)

Evaluate the PERT Techniques

Three estimates are produced for each activity

Most likely time (m), Optimistic time (a), Pessimistic (b) Expected time 't_e' = (a + 4m + b)/6

Activity Standard deviation 's' = (b-a)/6

Expected time: Helps to carry out a forward pass through a network similar to CPM Activity standard deviation: Used as a ranking measure of the degree of uncertainty or risk for each activity. Some straightforward activities (data input of standing data) might have little uncertainty and therefore have a low standard deviation, while others (software design) have uncertainty and would have a bigger standard deviation.

A Chain of Activities

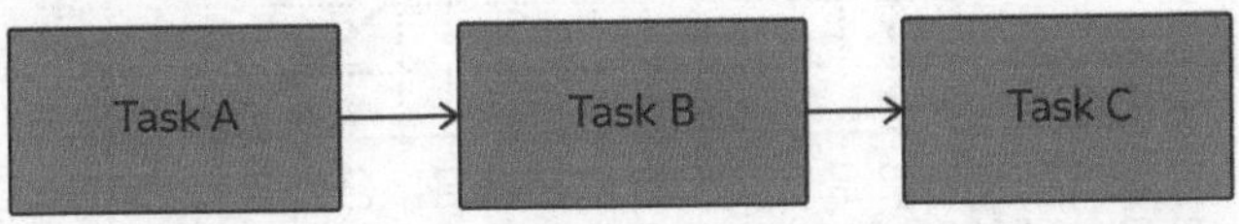

Task	a	m	b	t_e	s
A	10	12	16	?	?
B	8	10	14	?	?
C	20	24	38	?	?

Task A t_e = (10+ (12 x 4) + 16)/ 6 i.e. 12.66 s = (16-10)/6

i.e. 1

Task B t_e = (8 + (10 x 4) + 14)/ 6 i.e. 10.33 s = (14-8)/6 i.e. 1

Task C T_e = (20 + (24 x 4) + 38)/6

i.e. 25.66 s = (38-20)/6

i.e. 3

What would be the expected duration of the chain A + B + C?

Answer: 12.66 + 10.33 + 25.66

i.e. 48.65

What would be the standard deviation for A + B + C?

Answer: square root of ($1^2 + 1^2 + 3^2$)

i.e. 3.32.

Assessing the likelihood of meeting a target:

Say the target for completing A + B + C was 52 days (T)

Calculate the z value

$z = (T - t_e)/s$

In this example z = (52-48.33)/3.32

i.e. 1.01

Look up in the table of z values – see the next overhead. The target, in this case 52 days, is one that could be based on an externally imposed deadline e.g. the start of the London Olympics. The standardized calculation in Excel can be used to calculate the z value.

Graph of z values

There is about a 15% chance of not meeting the target of 52 days. The Excel normsdist can be used to do this calculation.

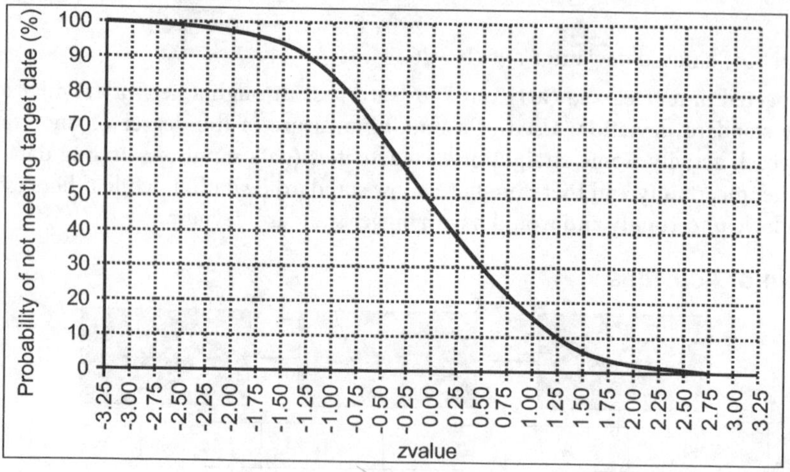

Figure 3.18.

PERT Labeling Convention

Event Number		Target Date			
Expected Date		Standard deviation			
Activ-ity	**Description**	**Precedents (s)**	**Optimistic (a)**	**Most likely (m)**	**Pessimistic (b)**
A	Hardware Selection		5	6	8
B	Software Design		3	4	5
C	Install Hardware	A	2	3	3
D	Code & test software	B	3.5	4	5
E	File take-on	B	1	3	4
F	Write user manuals		8	10	15
G	User training	E, F	2	3	4
H	Install and test	C,D	2	2	2.5

Monte Carlo Simulation

An alternative to PERT. A class of general analysis techniques:

Valuable to solve any problem that is complex, nonlinear, or involves more than a couple of uncertain parameters. Monté Carlo simulations involve repeated random sampling to compute the results.Gives realistic results as compared to manual approaches.A Monte Carlo method is a technique that involves using random numbers and probability to solve problems. Monte Carlo simulation is a method for iteratively evaluating a deterministic model using sets of random numbers as inputs. A simulation can involve over 10,000 evaluations of the model, a task which in the past was practical using supercomputers. The Monte Carlo method is one of many methods for analyzing uncertainty propagation, where the goal is to determine how random variation, lack of knowledge, or error affects the sensitivity, performance, or reliability of the system that is modeled. Monte Carlo simulation is categorized as a sampling method because the inputs are randomly generated from probability distributions to simulate the process of sampling from an actual population.We try to choose a distribution for the inputs that most closely matches data we already have, or best represents our current state of knowledge. The data generated from the simulation can be represented as probability distributions (or histograms) or converted to error bars, reliability predictions, tolerance zones, and confidence intervals.

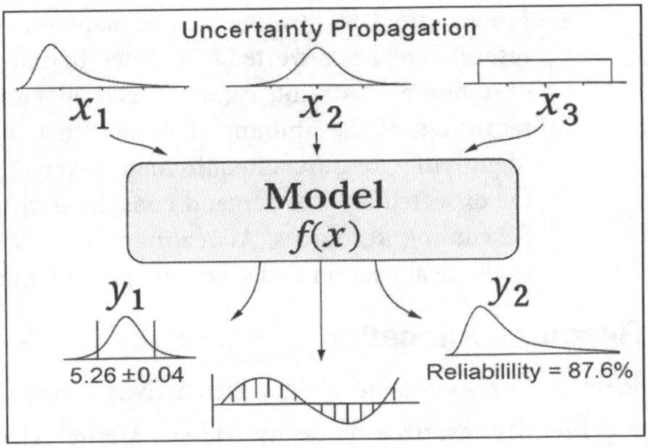

Figure 3.19.

The steps in Monte Carlo simulation corresponding to the uncertainty propagation shown in Figure are fairly simple, and can be easily implemented in Excel for simple models. All we need to do is follow the five simple steps listed below:

Step 1: Create a parametric model, y = f(x1, x2, ..., xq).

Step 2: Generate a set of random inputs, xi1, xi2, ..., xiq.

Step 3: Evaluate the model and store the results as yi.

Step 4: Repeat steps 2 and 3 for i = 1 to n.

Step 5: Analyse the results using histograms, summary statistics, confidence intervals, etc.

3.9 RESOURCE ALLOCATION AND NATURE OF RESOURCES

Resource allocation is the assignment of available resources to various uses. In the context of an entire economy, resources can be allocated by various means, such as markets or central planning. In project management, resource allocation or resource management is the scheduling of activities and the resources required by those activities while taking into consideration both the resource availability and the project time. Nature of Resources: These include

- **Labour:** Members of the project team
- **Equipment:** Workstations and other communicating and office equipment's
- **Material:** Items that are consumed
- **Space:** Office space
- **Services:** Some specialist services telecommunicating
- **Time:** Offset against the other primary resource. i.e., elapsed time can be reduced by adding staff.

- **Money:** used to buy the other resources, Money is the means by which one resource can be converted to another. In practice this may be problematic because of resource constraints e.g. staff need time to become expert in a new technology regardless of the amount of money that might be available to buy expertise. Identifying Resource Requirements. What resources are required along with the expected level of demand consider each activity Identify required resources. Scheduling Resources. Allocating resources for one activity limits flexibility for resource allocation and scheduling of other activities.

Resource Allocation

Identify the resources needed for each activity and create a resource requirement list.

Identify resource types: individuals are interchangeable within the group (e.g. VB programmers' as opposed to software developers'). Allocate resource types to activities and examine the resource histogram. For example, standard software developers have an average productivity. When we allocate actual people we may find that we have a trainee or a super-expert and this will affect productivity. A short-coming in productivity in an individual might be compensated for by a lower cost (as would be expected with trainees).

- **Priorities resource allocation:** Where more than one activity is competing for the same limited resource at the same time then those activities need to be prioritized. Two main ways:
  - **Total float priority:** Activities are ordered according to their total float. Those with the smallest float are assigned the highest priority.
  - **Ordered list priority:** Ordered according to predefined criteria. This takes account of the duration of the activity as well as the float see next overhead.

3.10 IDENTIFYING RESOURCE REQUIREMENTS AND SCHEDULING RESOURCES

Burman's Priority List

Give priority to the shortest critical path and critical activities, shortest non-critical activity and non-critical activity with least float. Non-critical activities map on activity plans to assess the distribution of resources required over the duration of the project Recruiting staff has cost. Smooth the histogram by delaying the start of some activities. Resource histogram: systems analysts. The resource histogram helps us identify where the demand for a resource exceeds the supply. If we use a tool such as MS Project, the tool will generate the resource histograms for us.

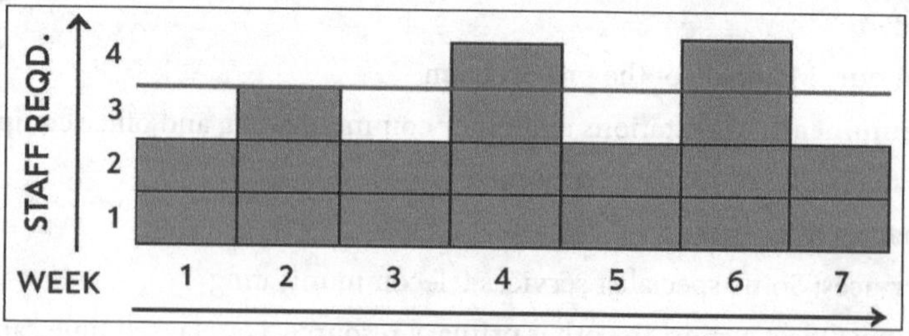

Figure 3.20.

Resource Smoothing

It is difficult to get specialist staff who will work odd days to fill in gaps – need for staff to learn about application etc.Staff have to be employed for a continuous block of time. Therefore desirable to employ a constant number of staff on a project – who as far as possible are fully employed. need for resource smoothing.

This shows an attempt to smooth the previous resource histogram. In order to do this, we have had to add another week to the schedule.Resource clashes where same resource needed in than one place at the same time can be resolved by delaying one of the activities taking advantage of float to change start date delaying start of one activity until finish of the other activity that resource is used on - puts back project completion moving resource from a on-critical activity bringing in additional resource - increases costs.Resource usage needs to maximize % usage of resources i.e. reduce idle periods between tasks need to balance costs against early completion date Need to allow for contingency.

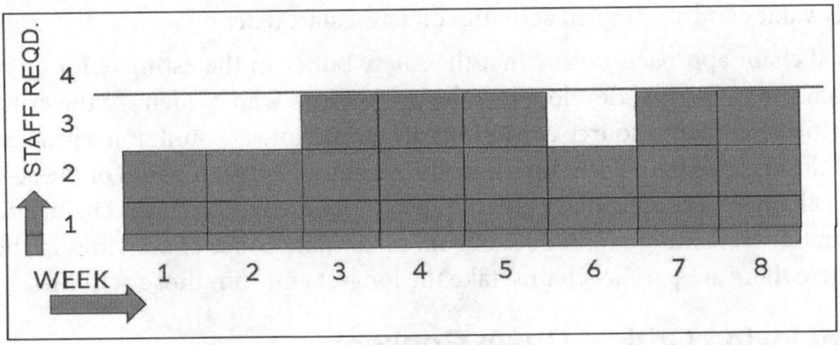

Figure 3.21.

Critical Path

Scheduling resources can create new dependencies between activities and recall critical chains. It is best not to add dependencies to the activity network to reflect resource constraints. Makes network very messy A resource constraint may disappear during the project, but link remains on network Amend dates on schedule to reflect resource constraints. The notation for activity networks does not tell you why one activity might be dependent on the completion of another.

Allocating Individuals to Activities

The initial resource types for a task have to be replaced by actual individuals. Factors to be considered Availability who is free Note that this will change during the course of the project as some tasks are completed earlier or later than planned. Criticality You would want to put your experienced, safer, staff on the critical activities. Risk this is similar to the point above, but some activities could be off the critical path but still have risks e.g. to the quality of subsequent products.

Training concerns about minimizing risk, it is healthy to take some risks in order to develop staff capabilities by allocating challenging tasks to relatively inexperienced staff. Team building and motivation identifying people who work well together can pay dividends; chopping and changing plans all the time may in theory optimize project performance, but can in practice be demotivating for staff.

3.11 CREATING CRITICAL PATHS AND COUNTING THE COST

Critical chain concept: Traditional planning approach:

This plan tends to start activities as early as possible for example see Activities E and H. While the float on these activities could be used as a buffer if they were late, other activities e.g. F. although of substantial duration do not have the same kind of cushion. In the case of F, the planner would have to make any safety buffer part of the core activity duration. One problem with estimates of task duration estimators is adding a safety zone to estimate to take account of possible difficulties. Developers work to the estimate + safety zone, so time is lost. No advantage is taken of opportunities where tasks can finish early and provide a buffer for later activities. Developers will tend to start activities as late as is compatible with meeting the target date as they have other urgent work to be getting on with in the meantime. Ask the estimators for two estimates Most likely duration: 50% chance of meeting this comfort zone additional time needed to have 95% chance. Schedule all activities using most likely values and starting all activities on latest start dates.

Critical chain approach means that the safety buffer in the estimate for an activity is moved from the individual developer to the project as a whole. Identify the critical chain –same a critical path but resource constraints also taken into account. Put a project buffer at the end of the critical chain with duration 50% of sum of comfort zones of the activities on the critical chain Where subsidiary chains of activities feed into critical chain, add feeding buffer. Duration of feeding buffer 50% of sum of comfort zones of activities in the feeding chain. Where there are parallel chains, take the longest and sum those activities.

Plan Employing Critical Chain Concepts

Executing the critical chain-based plan. No chain of tasks is started earlier than scheduled, but once it has started is finished as soon as possible. This means the activity following the current one starts as soon as the current one is completed, if this is early the relay race principle. Buffers are divided into three zones.

- **Green:** the first 33%. No action required
- **Amber:** the next 33%. Plan is formulated
- **Red:** last 33%. Plan is executed.

Schedules

Activity schedule: indicating start and completion dates for each activity

Resource schedule: indicating dates when resources needed + level of resources

Cost schedule: showing cumulative expenditure

Cost Schedule

Calculating cost is straightforward where the organization has standard cost figures for staff and other resources. Staff costs include not only salary, but social security funds, pension scheme contributions by the employer, holiday pay and sickness benefit etc. Cost schedules can be produced. Costs include:

- **Staff costs:** includes not just salary, but also social security contributions by the employer, holiday pay etc. Timesheets are often used to record actual hours spent on each project by an individual. One issue can be how time when a staff member

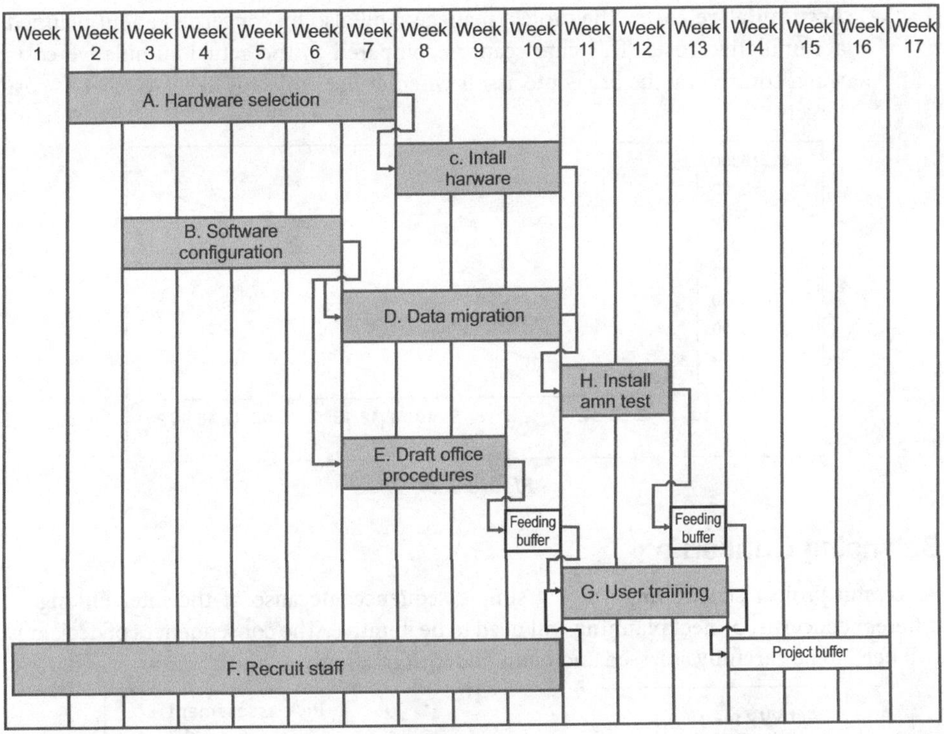

Figure 3.22.

is allocated and available to the project, but is not working on the project, is dealt with.

- **Overheads:** represents expenditure that an organization e.g. space rental, service charges etc. Some overheads might be directly attributable to the project, in other cases a percentage of departmental overheads may be allocated to project costs.
- **Usage charges:** projects are charged directly for use of resources such as computer time. Some charges can be on a pay as you go 'basis e.g. telephone charges, postage, car mileage at the planning stage an estimate of these may have to be made.

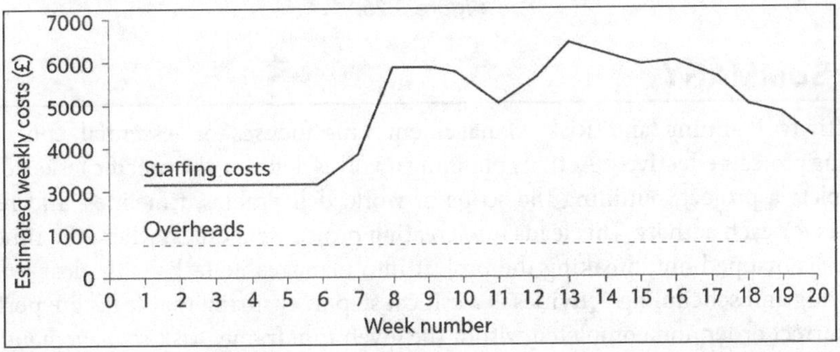

Figure 3.23.

This shows how much is going to be spent each week. This could be important where an organization allocates project budgets by financial year or quarter and the project straddles more than one of these financial periods.

- **Accumulative costs:** The project manager will also be concerned about planned accumulative costs. This chart can be compared to the actual cumulative costs when controlling the project to assess whether the project is likely to meet its cost targets.

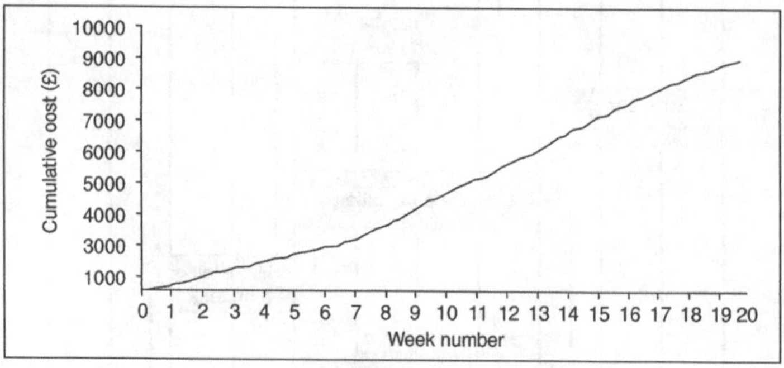

Figure 3.24.

Balancing Concerns

Successful project scheduling is not a simple sequence. Because of the inter-linking of different concerns, project planning will need to be iterative. The consequences of decisions will need to be carefully assessed and plans added accordingly.

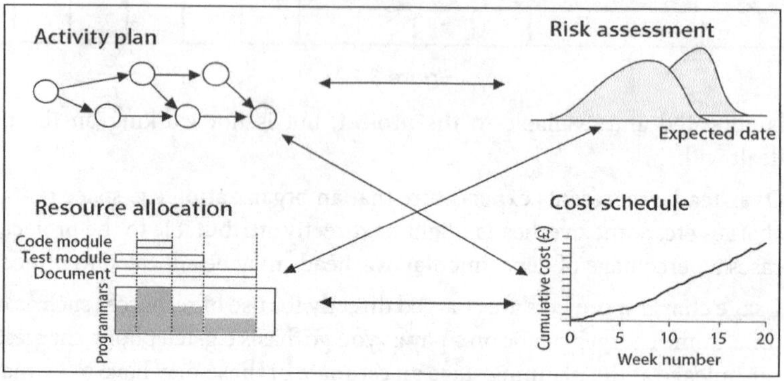

Figure 3.25.

UNIT SUMMARY

The Activity Planning and Risk Management unit focuses on essential concepts for managing projects effectively. Activity planning involves defining the specific tasks necessary to complete a project, outlining the scope of work, deliverables, timelines, and required resources for each activity. This leads into creating project schedules, where the timeline of activities is mapped out, breaking the project into manageable tasks with clear timelines. Sequencing and scheduling activities is a critical step in ensuring that tasks are performed in the correct order and completed within the given timeframe. Risk management plays a central role in the unit, focusing on the process of identifying, assessing, and mitigating risks throughout the project's life cycle. Additionally, the unit covers the creation of critical paths, which identify the sequence of tasks that dictate the project's overall timeline. Counting the cost involves estimating the financial resources needed for each task to ensure that the project stays within budget. Overall, this unit emphasizes the importance of detailed planning, effective scheduling, and proactive risk management in ensuring that projects are completed on time, within budget, and with minimal disruption. By properly allocating resources and managing risks, project managers can enhance their ability to deliver successful outcomes.

EXERCISES

1. What is the importance of activity planning in project management?
2. Describe the relationship between projects and activities. How do activities fit into a larger project?
3. Explain how project schedules are created and what factors need to be considered when developing a schedule.
4. Why is risk management an essential part of project planning and execution?
5. What are the key components of a risk management framework, and how do they help mitigate potential project risks?
6. List and explain the different types of risks that could arise in a project (e.g., schedule risks, financial risks, resource risks).
7. How would you identify risks in a project, and what tools or methods can be used in the risk identification process?
8. How do you develop strategies to mitigate or avoid risks in a project? Provide examples of risk management strategies.
9. In the event of a risk materializing, what steps should be taken to minimize its impact on the project's objectives?
10. How do you monitor and track risks throughout the project lifecycle to ensure the effectiveness of risk management strategies?

UUU

UNIT 4

Monitoring and Control

RATIONALE

Monitoring and control are essential for ensuring software projects stay on track. This unit covers progress tracking, cost monitoring, and earned value analysis to assess performance. Effective project management requires reviewing data, prioritizing tasks, and making necessary adjustments to meet targets. Additionally, software configuration management, contract handling, and people management play key roles in maintaining quality and efficiency. Understanding organizational behavior, selecting the right personnel, and implementing best practices enhance team productivity. Concepts like the Oldham-Hackman job characteristics model and stress management help create a balanced work environment, ensuring project success.

OUTCOMES

- Understand the importance of monitoring and control in project management.
- Apply earned value analysis for cost and progress tracking.
- Develop strategies to bring projects back on target when deviations occur.
- Learn software configuration management and contract management principles.
- Manage human resources effectively within a software environment.
- Analyze organizational behavior and employee motivation techniques.
- Implement stress management strategies to improve team productivity.

4.1 MONITORING AND CONTROL AND CREATING THE FRAMEWORK

Creating the Framework

Exercising control over a project and ensuring that targets are met is a matter of regular monitoring, finding out what is happening, and comparing it with current targets. If there is a mismatch between the planned outcomes and the actual one then either preplanning is needed to bring the project back on target or the target will have to be revised.

- **Define objectives:** at the beginning of the project we decide on what we want to achieve
- **Making decisions/plans:** we decide how we are going to achieve the objectives i.e. we create a plan
- **Modelling:** as part of the process of creating a plan we will consider different approaches and attempt to assess the consequences of each of these approaches in terms of how much it will cost and how long it will take, and so on.

A model of the project control cycle:

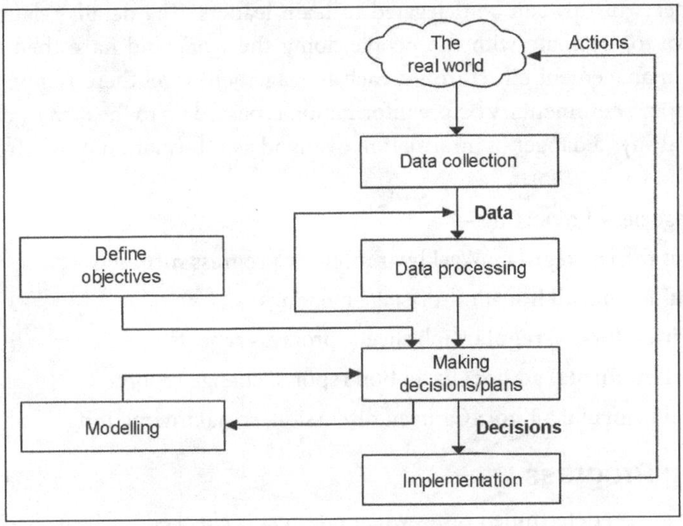

Figure 4.1.

Implementation – The Plan is Carried Out

- **Data collection:** we gather information at regular intervals about how the project is progressing. These raw details could be numerous and complex on a large project.
- **Data processing:** we process the progress data and convert it into information which makes it easier for the project managers and others to understand the overall condition of the project.
- **Making decisions/plans:** in the light of the comparison of actual project progress with that planned the plans are modified. This may require the modelling of the outcomes of different possible courses of action and so the cycle goes on.

Responsibilities

Overall responsibility of ensuring satisfactory progress on a project is the role of the project steering committee.

Figure illustrates the typical reporting structure found with medium and large projects

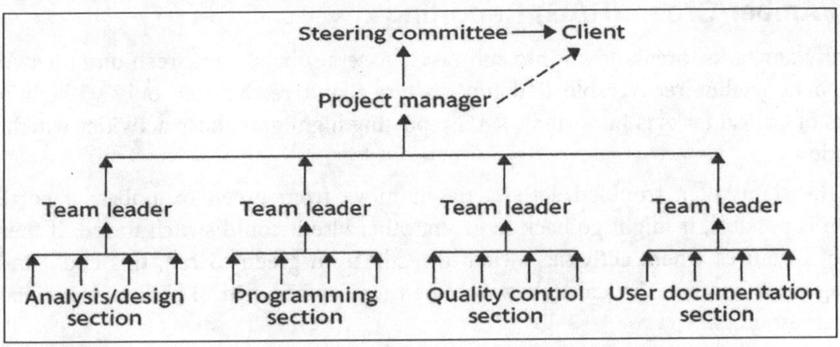

Figure 4.2.

Day to day responsibility will rest with the project manager and all in but the smallest projects, aspects of this can be delegated to team leaders. The details relating to project progress have to originate with the people doing the work and have then to be fed up through the management structure. At each management level there is going to be some summarising and commentary before information is passed up to the next level. This means that there is always a danger of information overload as information passes from the many to the few.

The categories of reporting—

- **Oral formal regular:** Weekly or monthly progress meetings
- **Oral formal ad hoc:** End-of-stage meetings
- **Written formal regular:** job sheets, progress reports
- **Written formal ad hoc:** Exception reports, change reports
- **Oral informal ad hoc:** Canteen discussion, social interaction

Assessing Progress

Checkpoints are predetermined times when progress is checked t driven check takes place when a t has been achieved Time driven: date of the check is predetermined.Frequency of reporting The higher the management level then the longer the gaps between checkpoints. Collecting progress details.

Need to collect data about: Achievements/ Milestones and Costs. A big problem: How to deal with partial completions? 99% completion syndrome Projects have to be delivered on time and within budget, the concern with monitoring achievements and costs.Partial completion is where, for example, data is collected at the end of Week 2 of an activity that should take four weeks.

We want to know if it is about 50% completed. An example of the '99% completion syndrome' would be in the above case if the developer reported at the end of weeks 1,2 and 3 that the task was respectively 25%, 50% and 75% complete. At the end of week 4 it is reported that the task is 99% complete. The same thing is reported at the end of week 5 and so on until the task is completed.

Possible solutions are control of products, not activities subdivided into lots of sub-activities control on products implies that actual examination of intermediate allows us to verify independently and objectively that subtasks have been completed.

Red/Amber/Green (RAG) Reporting

Identify key tasks, break down into sub-tasks, Assess subtasks as Green on target Amber not on target but recoverable Red not on target and recoverable only with difficulty. Status of critical tasks is important. RAG reporting highlights those activities which need attention.

The status of a troubled activity might move from green to amber; if corrective action is possible, it might go back to green, otherwise it could switch to red. If there are lots of instances where activities switch directly from green to red, this could indicate management control. Critical tasks would be those on the critical path and/or reliant on critical resources.

4.2 COLLECTING THE DATA AND REVIEW

Review of work products is an important mechanism for monitoring the progress of a project and ensuring the quality of the work products. Testing is an effective defect removal mechanism. Testing is applicable to only executable code. Review is applicable to all work products.

Utility of Review

A cost-effective defect removal mechanism. Review helps to identify any deviation from standards. Reviewers suggest ways to improve the work product. A review meeting provides learning opportunities to not only the author of a work product, but the other participants of the review meeting.The review participants gain a good understanding of the work product under review, making it easier for them to interface or use the work product in their work.

Review Roles

- **Moderator:** Schedules and convenes meetings, distributes review materials, leads and moderates review sessions.
- **Recorder:** Records the defects found and the time and effort data.
- Reviewers.

Collecting the Data Project Termination

Project Termination Review: Project termination reviews provide important opportunities to learn from past mistakes as well as successes. Project termination need not mean project failure or premature abandonment. A project may be terminated on successful completion.

Reasons for Project Termination

Project is completed successfully handed over to the customer. Incomplete requirements. Lack of resources. Some key technologies used in the project have become obsolete during project execution. Economics of the project has changed, for example because many competing products may have become available in the market. Project Termination Process are Project survey, Collection of objective information, Debriefing meeting, Final project review, Result publication.

4.3 VISUALIZING PROGRESS AND COST MONITORING

Collected data about project progress, a manager needs some way of presenting that data to greatest effect.

Gantt Chart

One of the simplest and oldest techniques for tracking project progress.An activity bar chart indicating scheduled activity dates and durations.Reported progress is recorded on the chart by shading activity bars.Today cursor provides visual indication of which activities are ahead or behind schedule. In fig., Code and test module D & Code and test module A- ahead of schedule. Code and test module B & Code and test module C – behind the schedule.The format of the Gantt chart differs from the format used in Microsoft project as the activities for each team member are grouped together. You could input the details so that they came out in this format, but it would not occur automatically.

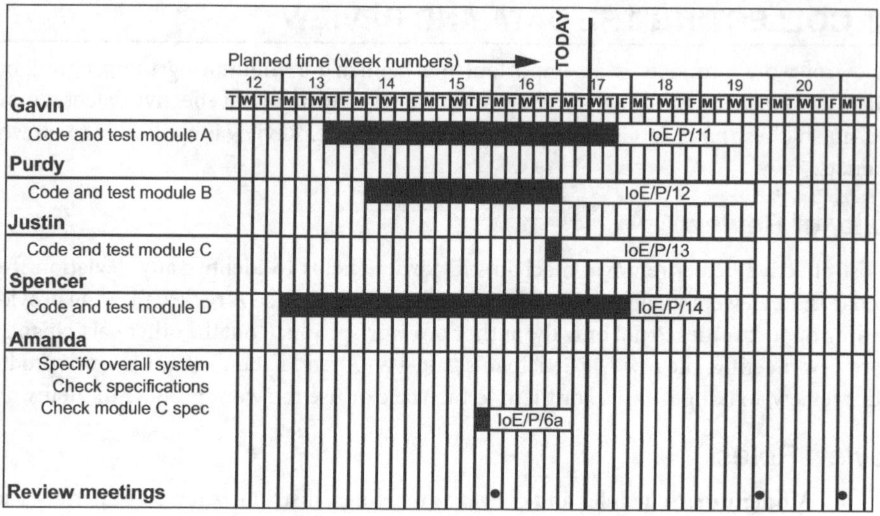

Figure 4.3.

Slip Chart

A slip chart is a version of the Gantt chart where a line is drawn from top to bottom. To the left of the line are all the completed activities and to the parts of activities that have not been completed. The jagged line means that there are some activities that are lagging to various degrees and some that are ahead of themselves. A very jagged line means that there is scope for re-planning to move resources from those activities that are ahead to those that are behind.

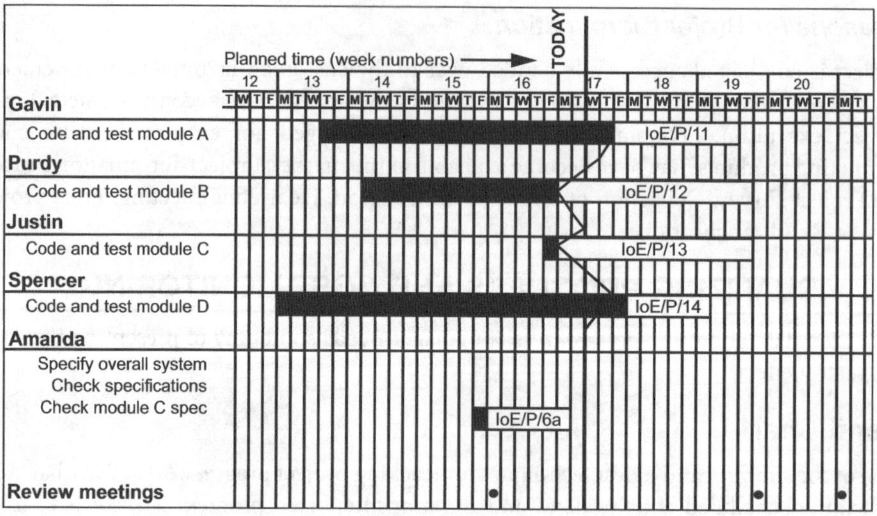

Figure 4.4.

A slip chart is a very similar alternative favored by some project managers who believe it provides a striking visual indication of those activities that are not progressing to schedule-the the slip line bends, the greater variation from the plan. Additional slip lines are added at intervals and as they build up the project manager will gain an idea as to whether the project is improving or not.A very jagged slip line indicates a need for rescheduling.

Timeline

The timeline chart is a method of recording and displaying the way in which targets have changed throughout the duration of the project. Planned time is plotted along the horizontal axis and elapsed time down the vertical axis. The lines meandering down the chart represent scheduled completion dates Analyse existing system –scheduled to be completed by Tuesday of week 3. Obtain user requirements- by Thursday of week 5 Issue tender- Tuesday of week 9. Review target dates. At the end of the first week review these targets dates and leaves them as they are (lines are drawn vertically downwards from the target dates to the end of week 1. At the end of week 2 he decides Obtain user requirements will not be completed until Tuesday of week 6 (extends the activity line diagonally). The other activity targets are delayed correspondingly. By the Tuesday of week 3 Analyse existing system is completed and he puts a blob on the diagonal timeline. At the end of week 4 he adds another 3 days to draft, render and issue tender. At the end of week 6 two activities have been completed.

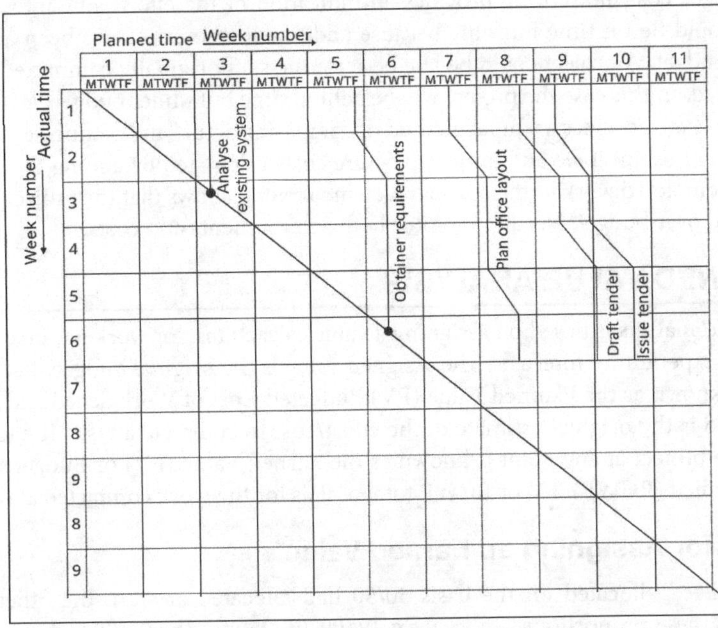

Figure 4.5.

This records the way that targets have changed throughout the project. Planned time is plotted on the horizontal axis, and actual time on the vertical axis. The bendy lines going from top to bottom represent the scheduled completion date for each activity. E.g. analyse existing system at start this was due finish on the Monday of week 3 and it did finish then obtain user requirements' was planned to finish on the Thursday of week 5, but at the end of the first week it was rescheduled to finish on the Tuesday of week 6.

Ball Chart

Shows whether or not targets have been met. Circles indicate estimated and actual start and completion points for activities Estimated start date for code and test module B: 6/4/99. Its Actual start date: 8/4/99.Estimated completion date for code and test module B: 13/5/99 Its Actual completion date: 17/5/99.

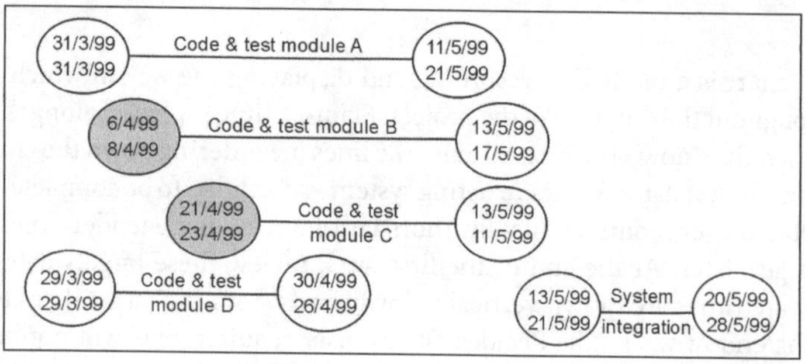

Figure 4.6.

Cost Monitoring

Expenditure or cost monitoring provides an indication of the effort gone into a project. A project could be on time but only because additional resources have been added and so by over budget. A project could be late because the staff originally committed have not been deployed. In this case the project will be behind time but under budget. A cumulative expenditure chart provides a simple method of comparing actual and planned expenditure. Cost charts are useful if we add projected future costs calculated by adding the estimated costs of uncompleted work to the costs already incurred. It shows that the project is behind schedule and over budget. Need to monitor both achievements and costs.

4.4 EARNED VALUE ANALYSIS

Earned value analysis is based on assigning a value to each task or work package based on the original expenditure forecasts. The assigned value is the original budgeted cost for the item and is known as the Planned Value (PV) Budgeted Cost of Work Scheduled (BCWS). PV or BCWS is the original estimate of the effort/cost to complete a task. The total value credited to a project at any point is known as the Earned Value (EV) or Budgeted Cost of Work Performed (BCWP). EV or BCWP total of PVs for the work completed at this time.

Methods for Assigning an Earned Value

Work completed allocated on the basis 50/50 half allocated at start, the other half on completion. These proportions can vary e.g. 0/100, 75/25 etc. The 0/100 technique: where a task is assigned a value of zero until that is completed when it is given a value of 100%. The 50/50 technique: where a task is assigned a value of 50% until that is completed when it is given a value of 50%.The 75/25 technique: where a task is assigned a value of 75% until that is completed when it is given a value of 25%.The milestone technique: Where a task is given a value based on the achievement of milestones. The percentage complete: where a task is given a value based on the amount of work completed. It can use money values, or staff effort as a surrogate.The baseline budget is the first stage in setting up an EVA is to create the baseline budget.The baseline budget is based on the project plan and shows the forecast growth in EV through time. EV may be measured in terms of monetary values, person-hours or workdays. Monitoring the Earned Value Having created the baseline budget, the next task is to monitor EV as the project progresses. This is done by monitoring the completion of tasks. The actual cost of each task can be collected as Actual Cost (AC) or Actual Cost of Work Performed (ACWP).

Performance Statistics

Scheduled variance: The schedule variance is measured in cost terms as EV-PV and indicates the degree to which the value of completed work differs from that planned. The difference between the Work Performed (BCWP) and the Work Scheduled (BCWS)

Time Variance (TV) is the difference between time when the achievement of the current EV was planned to occur and the time now. TV is the difference between time when specified EV should have been reached and time it was.

For example say an EV of £19000 was supposed to have been reached on 1st April and it was reached on 1st July then TV = –3 months. Cost variance is the difference between the planned Cost of Work Performed (BCWP) and actual cost incurred for the work (ACWP). Performance ratio

Cost Performance Index: CPI = EV/AC

The ratio of cost of work performed (BCWP) to actual cost (ACWP). CPI of 1.0 implies that the actual cost matches to the estimated cost. CPI greater than 1.0 indicates work is accomplished for less cost than what was planned or budgeted. CPI less than 1.0 indicates the project is facing cost overrun.

Schedule Performance Index: SPI= EV/PV.

The ratio of work accomplished (BCWP) versus work planned (BCWS), for a specific time period. SPI indicates the rate at which the project is progressing. SPI is more than 1, indicating that the project is ahead of schedule.

Earned value an example

Tasks

Specify module	5 days
Code module	8 days
Test module	6 days

At the beginning of day 20, PV = 19 days

If everything but testing completed EV = 13 days

Schedule variance = EV-PV i.e. 13 – 19 = –6

Schedule performance indicator (SPI) = 13/19 = 0.68

SV negative or SPI <1.00, project behind schedule In previous example, if Specify module 'took 3 day's Code module 'took 4 days'.

Actual cost = 7 days

Cost variance (CV) = EV–AC i.e. 13 – 7 = 6 days

Cost performance indicator = 13/7 = 1.86

Positive CV or CPI > 1.00 means project within budget. CPI can be used to produce new cost estimate

Budget At Completion (BAC) – current budget allocated to total costs of project.

Estimate At completion (EAC) – updated estimate = BAC/CPI

e.g. say budget at completion is £19,000 and CPI is 1.86

EAC = BAC/CPI = £10,215 (projected costs reduced because work completed in less time)

Example: Suppose a project is to be completed in one year at the cost of 1,00,000. After three months, you realize that the project is 30% complete at a cost of 40000. Assess the performance of the project.

PV= planned percentage completion of work × budgeted cost = 25% × 100000 = 25000 EV=percentage work completed × budgeted cost = 30 % × 100000 = 30000

CPI = EV/Actual cost incurred = EV/AC = 30000/40000 = 0.75 SPI = EV/PV = 30000/25000 = 1.2

Since CPI is less than 1, the project is over budget. SPI is more than 1, indicating that the project is ahead of schedule. At this rate the project will be delivered ahead of schedule but is over budget. Therefore, corrective action needs to be taken.

4.5 PRIORITIZING MONITORING

Types of Activity

Critical path activities: if these are late then the project as a whole will be delayed. Activities with no free float: A project with no free float will delay following dependent activities, although the project end date may not be directly threatened.

- **Activities with less than a specified float:** The projects when executed can be very dynamic: some activities will take longer than estimated others less; this could lead to the critical shifting. Activities with small floats are the most likely to find themselves turned into activities on the critical path if their floats get eroded.
- **High risk activities:** If the standard deviation for an activity is large, this indicates that there is a lot of uncertainty about how long it will take.
- **Activities using critical resources:** Some resources may only be available for a limited period and if the activities that need the resource are delayed the resource could become unavailable.

Getting back on track: options

Renegotiate the deadline if not possible then one way is to divide the deliverables into tranches delivering the ones most valuable to the client on or before the deadline, but delaying fewer valuable ones.

Try to shorten activities on critical path

e.g. Work overtime

Re-allocate staff from less pressing work by adding staff. Some activities lend themselves to this readily than others – it is difficult to do this with software development. It increases costs.

Reconsider activity dependencies: Over-lap the activities so that the start of one activity does not have to wait for completion of another allowing activities to overlap increases the risk of quality shortfalls split activities. **Exception planning:**

Some changes could affect Users The business case (e.g. costs increase reducing the potential profits of delivered software product). These changes could be to Delivery date, Scope and Cost.

First Stage

Write an exception report for sponsors (through project board)

Explaining problems

Setting out options for resolution

Second Stage

Sponsor selects an option (or identifies another option). Project manager produces an exception plan implementing selected option. Exception plan is reviewed and accepted/rejected by sponsors/Project Board.

4.6 GETTING THE PROJECT BACK TO TARGET

The Role of Configuration Librarian

Identifying items that need to be subject to change control: It is unlikely, for example that a feasibility report would be subject to change control once agreement has been obtained to start the project. Management of a central repository of the master copies of software and documentation. **Administering change procedures:** Someone ensures that there is adherence to change control procedures. **Maintenance of access records:** A situation to be avoided is where two different developers are making changes to the same software component.

Typical Change Control Process

One or users might perceive the need for a change. User management decide that the change is valid and worthwhile and pass it to development management. A developer is assigned to assess the practicality and cost of making the change. Development management report back to user management on the cost of the change; user management decide whether to go ahead and the user community itself must come to a consensus about whether a proposal for a change should go forward. A change deemed desirable by one part of the user community could cause opposition with other users. This part of the process involves a multipart form, initially raised by a user representative and then completed with a response by the developers. There could be a change control board with user and developer representatives that oversees this decision-making process. One or more developers are authorized to make copies of components to be modified: The configuration librarian would control this release. Copies modified. After initial testing, a test version might be released to users for acceptance testing. i.e., it is a copy that is modified; the original would still exist as the current operational version. When users are satisfied then operational release authorized – master configuration items updated. i.e., the previous version of the configuration items would be archived but preserved. If there are unforeseen problems with the new version when it is made operational then a fall-back to the previous version could be considered.

Change Control and Configuration Management

- **Change control:** Set of procedures to ensure that changes made only after a consideration of the full impacts.

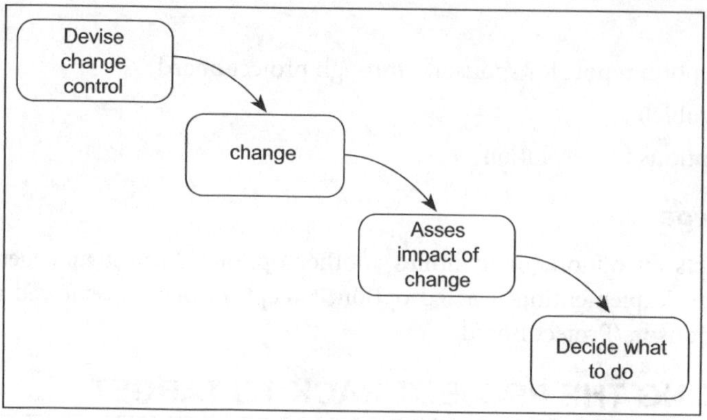

Figure 4.7.

- **Configuration management:** Version control to ensure that all changes are properly recorded and managed so that knock-on effects on other projects can be identified.

4.7 SOFTWARE CONFIGURATION MANAGEMENT

Throughout development, software consists of a collection of items (such as programs, data and documents) that can easily be changed. During software development, the design, code, and requirements are changed, and the changes occur at any time during the development. This easily changeable nature of software and the fact that changes take place require that changes be done in a controlled manner. Software Configuration Management (SCM) is the discipline for systematically controlling the changes that take place during developments is a process independent of the development process largely because most development models cannot accommodate change at any time during development. SCM is concerned with tracking and controlling changes to software.

Development and Maintenance Environment

Various work products associated with the software continually change. Unless a proper configuration management system is deployed, several problems can appear.

SCM Three Major Components

Software configuration identification, Change control and Status accounting and auditing.

1. Configuration Identification

The first requirement for any change management is to have clearly agreed-on basis for change. That is, when a change is done, it should be clear to what changes has been applied. This requires baselines to be established. A baseline change is the changing of the established baseline, which is controlled by SCM. After baseline changes the state of the software is defined by the most recent baseline and the changes that were made. Some of the baselines are functional or requirements baseline, design baseline, and product or system baseline. Functional or requirement baseline is the requirements document that specifies the functional requirements for the software. Design baseline consists of the different components in the software and their designs. Product or system baseline represents the developed system. A baseline is established after the product is relatively stable. Though the goal of SCM is to control the establishment and changes to these baselines, treating each baseline as a single unit for the purpose of change is undesirable, as the change may be limited to a very small portion of the baseline.

2. Change Control

Most of the decisions regarding the change are taken by the Configuration Control Board (CCB), which is a group of people responsible for Configuration Management (CM), headed by the configuration manager. For smaller projects, the CCB might consist of one person. Two main operations: Reserve and Restore.

A change is initiated by a Change Request (CR). The reason for change can be anything. The common reasons are requirement changes, changes due to bugs, platform changes, and enhancement changes. The CR for change consists of three parts:

The first part describes the change, reason for change, the SCIs that are affected, the priority of the change, etc.

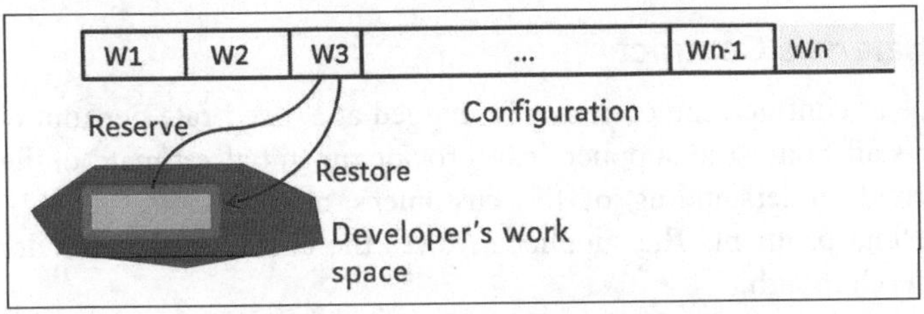

Figure 4.8.

The second part, filled by the CM, describes the decision taken by the CCB on this CR, the action the CM feels need to be done to implement this change and any other comments the CM may have.

The third part is filled by the implementer, which later implements the change.

3. Status Accounting and Auditing

For status accounting, the main source of information is the CRs and FRs themselves. A field in the CR/FR is added that specifies its current status. The status could be active, complete, or not scheduled. Information about dates and efforts can be added to the CR, the information from the CRs/FRs can be used to prepare a summary, which can be used by the project manager and the CCB to track all the changes.

4.8 MANAGING CONTRACTS AND MANAGING PEOPLE IN SOFTWARE ENVIRONMENT

Acquiring software from external supplier

This could be a bespoke system created especially for the customer off-the-shelf - bought as is customised Off-The-Shelf (COTS) a core system is customized to meet needs of a customer.

Types of Contracts

One way of classifying contracts is by the way that the payment to suppliers is calculated. They are fixed price contracts– Time and materials contracts. Fixed price per delivered unit contracts. License to use software is bought rather than the software itself.

Fixed Price Contracts

As the name implies, in this situation a price is fixed when the contract is signed. The customer knows that, if there are no changes in the contract terms, this is the price to be paid on the completion of the work. In order for this to be effective, the customer's requirement has to be known and fixed at the outset. In other words when the contract is to construct a software system, the detailed requirements analysis must already have been carried out. Once the development is under way the customer cannot change their requirement without renegotiating the price of the contract though the supplier will have to add a margin to the price to deal with contingencies, the cost could still be less than doing the work in-house as the supplier may be able to exploit economies of scale and the expertise that they have from having done similar projects in the past. When competing for work, there will be pressure on the suppliers to reduce prices. Once a contract has been won and signed, the contractor is in a stronger negotiating position when it comes to negotiating the price of additional work as the customer is locked in.

Time and Materials Contract

With this type of contract, the customer is charged at a fixed rate per unit of effort, for example, per staff-hour. The supplier may provide an initial estimate of the cost based on their current understanding of the customer's requirements, but this is not the basis for the final payment. The supplier invoices the customer for work done at regular intervals, say each month.

Fixed Price per Unit Delivered Contract

This is associated with Function Point (FP) counting. The size of the system to be delivered is calculated or estimated at the outset of the project. The size of the system to be delivered might be estimated in lines of code, but FPs can be easily derived from requirements document. A price per unit is quoted. The final price is then the unit price multiplied by the number of units it delivered contracts. Table shows typical prices:

FP count	Function design cost per FP	Implementation cost per FP	Total cost per FP
Upto 2000	$242	$725	$967
2001-2500	$255	$764	$1019
2501-3000	$265	$793	$1058
3001-3500	$274	$820	$1094
3501-4000	$284	$850	$1134

These figures do come from a real source (RDI Technologies in the USA). These are several years old. The bigger the project, the higher the cost per function point.

Fixed price/unit example: Estimated system size 2,600 FPs Price

2000 FPs × $967 plus 500 FPs × $1,019 plus 100 FPs × $1,058

i.e. charge for 2600 FPs =$2,549,300

What would be charge for 3,200 FPs? × 2000 FPs at $967 = $1,934,000

500 FPs at $1019 = $509,500

500 FPs at $1058 = $529,000

200 FPs at $1094= $218,800

Charge for 3,200 FPs = $3,191,300

Charging for Various Cases

- **Case 1:** For example, a system to be implemented contains 2600 FPs. The overall charges would be 2000 × 967 + 500 × 1019 + 100 ×1058 = $2,549,300.
- **Case 2:** The software supplier may carry out the system design. A charge could then make for design work based on column 2.

  For example, if the designed system was counted at 1000 FPs. It would be 1000 × 242. If the design was implemented and the actual software delivered, additionally 1000 × 725 would be charged.
- **Case 3:** If the scope of the system grows because the users find new requirements, new requirements would be charged at the combined rate for design and implementation. For example, 100 extra FPs were found, then the charge for this extra work = 100 × 967.

The Tendering Process

Another way of categorizing contracts is according to the approach that is used in contractor selection. They are Open tendering process, Restricted tendering process and Negotiated procedure.

Open Tendering Process

As there is no "pre-qualification" of bidders, anyone can submit a tender and it is possible that a large number of suppliers will bid. All bids compliant must be considered and evaluated in the same way any supplier can bid in response to the invitation to tender all tenders must be evaluated in the same way government bodies may have to do this by local/ international law (including EU and WTO, World Trade Organization, requirements).

Restricted Tendering Process

Consider the restricted procedure where you want to "pre-qualify" suppliers based on their financial standing and technical or professional capability so as to narrow the number permitted to submit bids only from those specifically invite can reduce suppliers considered at any stage.

Negotiated Procedure

The negotiated procedure can only be used in extremely limited circumstances. i.e., negotiate with one supplier e.g. for extensions to software already supplied. Typical indicators that the negotiated procedure with publication of a contract notice might be appropriate would be:

1. the contract is for a genuinely unique type of solution
2. the funding model is untested
3. the contracting authority is not aware of any other contracts using a similar model.

Legal advice should be sought before using the negotiated procedure and a note of why the procedure is used should be retained.

4.9 UNDERSTANDING BEHAVIOR AND ORGANIZATIONAL BEHAVIOR

Understanding Behavior

Identify the handling of people 2 approach:

Positivist approach is based on development of system. Discipline of Organizational behaviour theories "If A is the situation, then B is likely to result". Interpretivist approach. How software Engineer defined? Who customize and install package software it covers the role of ICT business analyst. How successful defined the 2 viewpoints (positivist and interpretivist) are both valid and useful in managing the people in software field.

Positivist Approach

Tends to be objective and empirical seeks causes for behaviour it conduct studies that can be generalised to larger populations interpretivist methodology qualitative based on smaller samples view each consumption situation as unique and non-predictive look for common patterns across consumption situations.

Organization Behaviour

The management's action of motivating human s in the organization, according to Douglas McGregor, involves certain assumptions, generalizations and hypotheses relating to human behavior and human nature. McGregor has characterized these assumptions in two opposite views, termed theory × and theory y.

Theory X

This is the traditional theory of human behaviour, In this theory, McGregor has certain assumptions about human behaviour. These assumptions are as follows:

- Management is a process of directing employees' efforts, motivating them, controlling their actions, modifying their behaviour to fit the needs of the organization.
- Without this active intervention by management, people would be passive resistant to organizational needs. They must be persuaded, rewarded, punished, controlled, and their activities must be directed. The average man is by nature indolent he works as little as possible.
- He lacks ambition, dislikes responsibility, prefers to be led. He is inherently self-centred, indifferent to organizational needs. He is, by nature, resistant to change. He is gullible, not very bright, the ready dupe of the charlatan and the demagogue. These assumptions about human nature are negative in their approach, much organisational processes have developed on these assumptions.

Theory Y

The assumptions of Theory Y are described by McGregor in the following words:

The expenditure of physical and mental effort in work is as natural as play or rest. The average human does not inherently dislike work. Depending upon controllable conditions, work may be a source of satisfaction or a source of punishment. External control and the threat of punishment are not the only means for bringing about effort towards organizational objectives. Man will exercise self-direction and self-control in the service of objectives to which he is committed. Commitment to objectives is a function of the reward associated with their achievement. The most significant of such awards, e.g. the satisfaction of ego and self-actualization needs, can be a direct product of effort directed towards organizational objectives. The average human learns under proper conditions not only to accept, but to seek responsibility. Avoidance of responsibility, lack of ambition, and emphasis on security are consequences of experience, not inherent human characteristics. The capacity to exercise a relatively high degree of imagination, ingenuity, and creativity in the solution of organizational problems is widely, not narrowly, distributed in the population. The assumptions of Theory Y suggest a new approach in management. It emphasizes on the cooperative endeavour of management and employees.

4.10 SELECTING THE RIGHT PERSON FOR THE JOB AND INSTRUCTION IN THE BEST METHODS

How do you select the right persons for the job?

There is no perfect answer, but the interview process can be a tremendous help if you use it effectively. In order, the key steps to finding the right person to fill a position in your company include is determining your need to hire a new employee. Conducting a thorough job analysis. Writing a job description and job specification for the position based on the job analysis. Determining the salary for the position, based on internal and external equity. Deciding where and how to find qualified applicants. Collecting and reviewing a fair number of applications and resumes and then selecting the most qualified candidates for further consideration. Interviewing the most qualified candidates for the position, based on the job's description and specification. Checking references and Hiring the best person for the job.

The Recruitment Process

It must be stressed that project leader have little choice about the people who will make up their team.

- **Create a job specification:** advice is needed as there could be legal implications in an official document.
- **Create a job holder profile:** it is used to construct a profile of the person needed to carry out the job.
- **Obtain applicants:** an advertisement would be placed, either within the organization in the trade. By giving the salary, location, job scope and any essential qualification, the applicants will be limited to the realistic candidates.
- **Examine CVS:** these should be read carefully and compared to the job holder profile nothing is annoying for all concerned than when people have cvs which indicate clearly that they are not eligible for the job and yet are called for interview. Selection techniques are aptitude, personality test and the examination of sample of previous work. Any method must test specific qualities detailed in the job holder profile. Interviews are the most used method. An interview might be of a technical nature where the practical expertise of the candidate is assessed.
- **Other procedures:** references will need to be taken up where necessary and a medical examination might be needed.

Steps

- **Initial Contact from the Client:** Based on the requirement, we assign the right recruitment consultant from day one that runs with the job until completion.
- **Job Specification:** First steps are all about information gathering and ensuring we receive a detailed job specification - if there is no job description available your recruitment consultant will work with you to understand the role profile and selection criteria.
- **Detailed brief:** Arras then understands the finer details of a job - the key drivers, ways of working and organizational ethos, the personality and softer skills needed for the job. All these details are shared with the candidate at shortlist stage to give them a fuller picture of the job.
- **Timescales and Process:** By outlining the recruitment timescales and preferred interview process with you; 1st, 2nd, 3rd interviews or assessment Centre, we can plan and manage expectations throughout the process with the shortlisted candidates. We aim to try and avoid those recruitment frustrations like waiting ages for feedback and interview shortlisting.
- **Search and selection:** The term used is the activities we perform to find the ideal candidates for the job. We encourage candidates to register with us - this is where most of our placed project management candidates originate from. The next step is to advertise on the project management job board. We then use a selection of methods both online (job boards, social media etc.) and offline (networking groups, press etc).
- **Arras One-to-One interview:** There is an initial screening project management interview with the recruitment consultant for each candidate for each role we recruit for. We have never shortlisted a candidate for a client without carrying out this interview-this works for both parties; we understand about a candidate's skills, experiences and suitably for the job whilst informing about the company and the opportunity they are interviewed for.
- **Shortlisting:** Following the project management interview candidates are asked if the role is something that they would like to pursue. Arras People only forward details of candidates to our clients when given expressed permission to do so. When in agreement, the consultant will send the candidate CV and an individual profile of skills, experience and capability for the job.
- **Interview management:** Once the client has reviewed the CV and profile candidates are notified when feedback is available. If a candidate is unsuccessful at this stage, the consultant will give feedback. Feedback obviously comes back in varying degrees of detail but we share everything we know. All candidates selected to attend an interview will be contacted by the consultant straight away with the details. With each interview, the consultant will arrange for an interview preparation session, helping candidates get ready for the interview by sharing details about the type of interview, who will be interviewing and any hints and tips which will be useful for that job and client. Interview preparation sessions are carried out for each interview regardless of how many stages. If interviews include a presentation - the consultant will walk through and review that.
- **Offers:** Each consultant at Arras is here to represent candidates through to the offer and negotiation stage. Following the successful interview candidates are contacted with feedback and the pending offer. By working closely with the Arras

consultant, candidates can be assured that the offer stage is managed effectively and smoothly to completion.

- **Start:** When details of offers and start dates are finalized, the Arras consultant remains in touch throughout. Arras will follow up with brief calls to make sure you are happy in your new job.

4.11 THE OLDHAMHACKMAN JOB CHARACTERISTICS MODEL AND STRESS MANAGEMENT

The job characteristics model, designed by Hackman and Oldham, is based on the idea that the task itself is keys to employee motivation. Specifically, a boring and monotonous job stifles motivation to perform well, whereas a challenging job enhances motivation. Variety, autonomy and decision authority are three ways of adding challenge to a job. Job enrichment and job rotation are the two ways of adding variety and challenge.

It states that there are five core job characteristics (skill variety, task identity, task significance, autonomy, and feedback) which impact three critical psychological states (experienced meaningfulness, experienced responsibility for outcomes, and knowledge of the actual results), in turn influencing work outcomes (job satisfaction, absenteeism, work motivation, etc.).

The five core job characteristics can be combined to form a motivating potential score (MPS) for a job, which can be used as an index of how likely a job is to affect an employee's attitudes and behaviors.

Hackman and Oldham's job characteristics theory proposes that high motivation is related to experiencing three psychological states whilst working:

- **Meaningfulness of work:** That labor has meaning to you, something that you can relate to, and does not occur as a set of movements to be repeated. This is fundamental to intrinsic motivation, i.e. that work is motivating of itself (as opposed to motivating only as a means to an end).
- **Responsibility:** That you have been given the opportunity to be a success or failure at your job because sufficient freedom of action has given you. This would include the ability to make changes and incorporate the learning you gain whilst doing the job.
- **Knowledge of outcomes:** This is important for two reasons. Firstly to provide the person knowledge on how successful their work has been which in turn enables them to learn from mistakes. The second is to connect them emotionally to the customer of their outputs, giving further purpose to the work (e.g. I may only work on a production line, but I know that the food rations I produce are used to help people in disaster areas, saving many lives).

Oldham and Hackman suggest that the satisfaction that the job gives is based on 5 factors.

- **Skill variety:** the number of different skills that the job holder has the opportunity to exercise.
- **Task identity:** the degree to which your work and its results are identifiable as belonging to you.
- **Task significance:** the degree to which your job has an influence on others
- **Autonomy:** the discretion you have about the way you to the job.

- **Feedback:** the information you get back about results of your work.

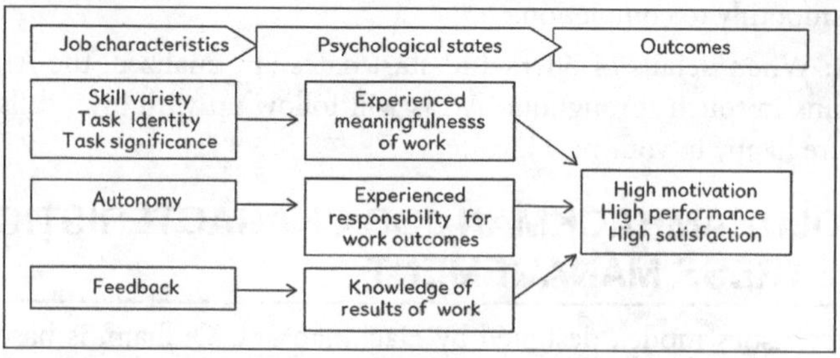

Figure 4.9.

Methods of Improving Motivation

- **Set specific goal:** These goals need to be demanding and yet acceptable to staff. Involving staff in the setting goal helps to gain acceptance for them.
- **Provide feedback:** Not only do goals have to be set but staff need regular feedback about how they are progressing.
- **Consider job design:** Jobs can be altered to make them interesting and give staff feeling of responsibility. Various measurements of job design– Simplification of Job: In job simplification jobs are broken in to very small parts as in assembly line operations and work can be ne by same individual repeatedly and it will increase productivity and proficiency of individual.
- **Job Enlargement:** Job enlargement expands job horizontally. It increases job scope; that is, it increases the number of different operations required in a job and the frequency with which the job cycle is repeated. By increasing the number of tasks an individual performs, job enlargement, increases the job scope, or job diversity.
- **Job Rotation:** Job rotation is the systematic and planned rotation of individuals in pre- determined jobs (other than their own) so they can gain additional knowledge or skills. It is done quite a bit for developing managers (because they need to be familiar with operations overall) and used with others who want to advance to a new role or become knowledgeable in their current job role.
- **Job Enrichment:** The job holder carries out that are done at a managerial or supervisory level. With programmers in a maintenance team, they may give authority to accept requests for changes that involve then five days's work without the need for their manager's approval. It is different from job enlargement (which focuses on increasing the number of tasks a job holder is responsible for performing work/tasks to do).

Stress Management

While some workplace stress can be considered normal, excessive workplace stress can interfere with employee productivity and it can have a negative impact on the physical and emotional health of the employee. Although it is evident that not everything in a work environment can be controlled, the good news is that stress can be managed. It does not involve making huge changes; rather it focuses on the one factor that can be controlled: the individual/the employee. Stress management is important to project managers because at this period competition is keener in many industries and it is important to learn new and better ways of dealing with the pressure at work as well as managing projects from start to finish.

Over the years, stress has been defined as strain within a person and as pressure from the environment. Today, the generally accepted definition of stress is seen as an interaction between the situation and the individual. Michie (2002) defines stress as the psychological and physical state that results when the resources of the individual are not sufficient to cope with the demands and pressures of the situation. This implies that stress is more likely to occur in some individuals than others and in some situations than others.

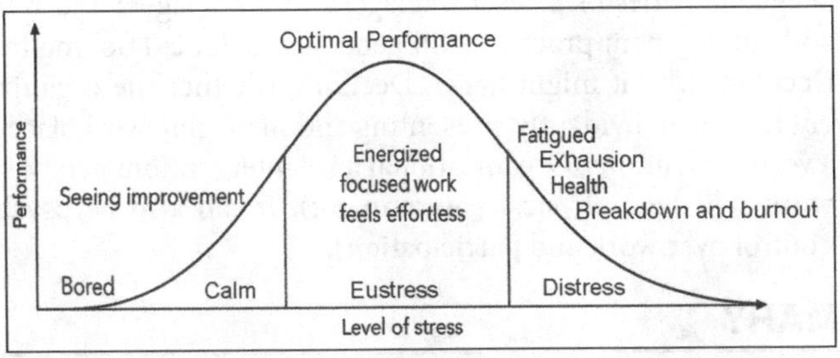

Figure 4.10.

The Yerlees-Dodson Curve

Based on the Yerkes-Dodson curve, moderate level of stress improves performance and when the stress level increases more, the performance decreases. Hence, it is crucial for project managers to be able to moderate the stress levels for optimal performance.

Causes of Stress at Work

Generally, and as it is presented above in the model, causes or sources of stress can be categorized into five categories.

Factors that are intrinsic to jobs:

- The role of the employee in the organization
- Career development issues
- Employee's relationship with others at work
- he structures and the climate of the organization
- The sources of stress identified above can be further put into two categories:
- Stress that has to do with the content of work
- Stress that is related to the social and organizational context of work

The model also shows that if stress persists, it can lead to mental and physical ill health. Empirical evidence shows that the common causes of stress at work include :

- Fear of being laid off
- Increased overtime caused by staff cutbacks
- Pressure to meet high expectations but with no increase in job satisfaction
- Pressure to work at optimal levels at all times

Situations that are likely to induce stress are those that are unpredictable or uncontrollable, unfamiliar or ambiguous, uncertain, loss of performance expectation and situations involving conflict. Time limited situations such as work deadlines, family demands, job insecurity and ongoing situations or projects also cause stress.

Historically, the typical response from employers has been to blame the stress victim rather than the cause of the stress. In recent times, it is increasingly being recognized that ensuring employee wellbeing is an important management responsibility. It is in the best interest of the organization to keep stress levels to a minimum for their long- term economic interest. In the absence of stress at the workplace, there is likely to be low employee turnover, reduction in sickness absence and early retirement, increased work performance, increased client satisfaction and reduced accident rate. An organization works to reduce stress through the strategic activities of project managers, line managers and human resources department. Good employment practices will generally include: Looking for the causes of stress at work Deciding who it might harm. Deciding whether the organization is doing enough to prevent the harm. Evidently, preventing and managing workplace stress requires organizational level interventions. Organizational level interventions can be structural (e.g., staffing levels, work schedule, physical environment). It can also be psychological (e.g., social support, control over work and participation).

UNIT SUMMARY

Monitoring and control in project management involves establishing a structured framework to track progress and ensure alignment with objectives. It begins with collecting data and reviewing performance metrics to analyze deviations and inform decision-making. Visualizing progress and cost monitoring through dashboards, reports, and charts help track time, budget, and scope adherence. A key technique, earned value analysis (EVA), compares planned versus actual costs and progress to assess project performance. Prioritizing monitoring ensures focus on critical areas, while getting the project back on track involves corrective actions to realign with goals. In software projects, software configuration management helps maintain integrity by controlling changes and versions. Managing contracts and people effectively ensures successful collaboration in software environments, supported by insights from organizational behavior to understand team dynamics. Selecting the right person for the job and providing effective instruction enhances workforce productivity. The Oldham-Hackman job characteristics model highlights job design principles to improve motivation, while stress management techniques help maintain a healthy work environment. Effective monitoring and control ensure project success by integrating technical oversight with strategic human resource management.

EXERCISE

1. What are the key components of an effective monitoring and control framework?
2. Why is data collection important in project monitoring, and what are some common data collection methods?
3. How does visualizing progress help in project management?
4. Explain the significance of cost monitoring in project success.
5. Define Earned Value Analysis (EVA) and explain its main components.
6. How does EVA help in assessing project performance?
7. What is software configuration management, & why is it important in software projects?
8. Discuss the key elements involved in managing software versions and changes.
9. Explain the Oldham-Hackman job characteristics model and its impact on motivation.
10. What are some effective stress management techniques in a work environment?

UUU

UNIT 5

Software Quality

RATIONALE

Software quality is essential for delivering reliable, efficient, and maintainable software products. This unit explores the importance of quality management, covering ISO 9126 quality models, product and process metrics, and quality management systems. Understanding process capability models and techniques for enhancing software quality ensures continuous improvement. Testing and software reliability play a crucial role in defect detection and prevention. Quality plans help organizations implement structured approaches to maintain high standards. By mastering these concepts, professionals can ensure software meets user expectations, complies with industry standards, and enhances overall project success.

OUTCOMES

- Understand the significance of software quality in project success.
- Define software quality and explore quality models such as ISO 9126.
- Differentiate between product and process quality management.
- Learn about quality management systems and process capability models.
- Apply techniques to enhance software quality and reliability.
- Understand software testing methods and their role in quality assurance.
- Develop and implement effective quality plans in software projects.

5.1 SOFTWARE QUALITY

The quality of software can be defined as the ability of the software to function as per user requirement. When it comes to software products it must satisfy all the functionalities written down in the SRS document.

Example: Consider a functionally correct software product. That is, it performs all tasks as specified in the SRS document. But, has an almost unusable user interface. Even though it may be functionally right, we cannot consider it to be a quality product.

In software quality engineering, engineers play a key role. Quality engineers design, implement, and maintain policies and procedures used to ensure the quality of development processes. This requires a thorough understanding of evaluation practices and technologies in use, including artificial intelligence (AI), big data analytics, and automation.

The quality of software can be defined as the ability of the software to function as per user requirement. When it comes to software products it must satisfy all the functionalities written down in the SRS document. Example: Consider a functionally correct software product. That is, it performs all tasks as specified in the SRS document. But, has an almost unusable user interface. Even though it may be functionally right, we cannot consider it to be a quality product. In software quality engineering, engineers play a key role. Quality engineers design, implement, and maintain policies and procedures used to ensure the quality of development processes. This requires a thorough understanding of evaluation practices and technologies in use, including artificial intelligence (AI), big data analytics, and automation.

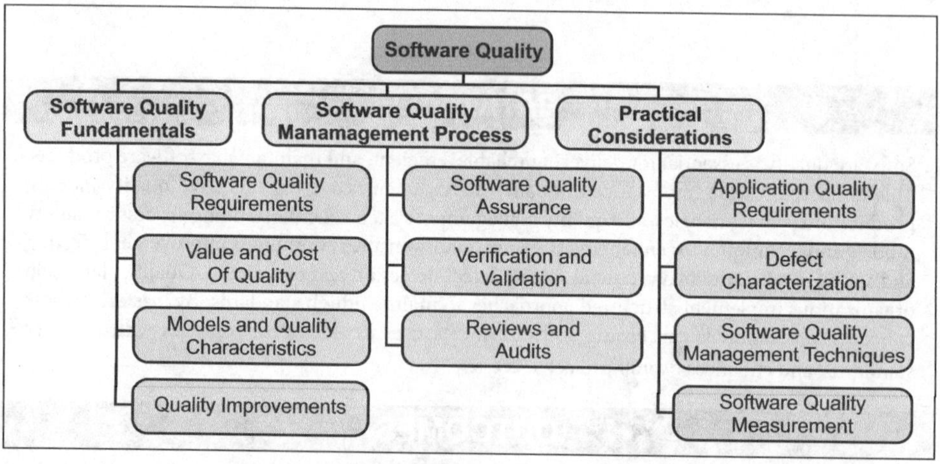

Figure 5.1.

One of the important issues that business has focused on in the last two decades is "quality". The other issues are cost and delivery. Quality has been widely considered as a key element for success in business in the present competitive market. Quality refers to meeting the needs and expectations of customers. It is important to understand that quality is about more than a product simply working properly.

Five Views of Software Quality

- **Product view:** If a product is manufactured with good internal characteristics, then it will have good external qualities. Quality is viewed as a quantifiable or measurable characteristics or attribute. But quality is based on individual taste or, the benchmark for measurement may be misleading.
- **User view:** In this view, the user is concerned with whether or not the product is fit for use. The product should meet user needs and expectations.
- **Manufacturing view:** In this view, quality is seen as conforming to requirements.
- **Value-Based view:** The central view in this case is how much a customer is willing to pay for a certain level of quality.
- **Transcendental view:** Quality is viewed to be something ideal. In this case, no effort is made to express it using concrete measures. Those who hold the transcendental view would say "I can't define it, but I know it when I see it". Advertisers are fond of promoting products in these terms. "Where shopping is a pleasure" (supermarket). "We love to fly and it shows" (airline).

5.2 IMPORTANCE OF SOFTWARE QUALITY

Software quality is crucial in ensuring that a software product meets user requirements, performs reliably, and operates efficiently. High-quality software enhances user satisfaction by providing a seamless and error-free experience, reducing frustration and improving overall usability. It also lowers maintenance costs, as fewer defects and issues result in reduced debugging, patching, and updates. Additionally, software quality is essential for security, as poor-quality software is more vulnerable to cyber threats, data breaches, and system failures.

From a business perspective, maintaining software quality boosts reputation and customer trust, leading to increased user retention and competitiveness in the market. It also helps in compliance with industry standards and regulations, ensuring that the software meets legal and ethical guidelines. Furthermore, high-quality software improves efficiency and performance, reducing system crashes and enhancing speed, responsiveness, and resource utilization.

In critical sectors such as healthcare, finance, and transportation, software quality can be a matter of life and death, making reliability and accuracy essential. By following best practices, rigorous testing, and continuous improvement processes, organizations can develop software that is robust, scalable, and future-proof, ultimately leading to better business outcomes and long-term success.

5.3 DEFINING SOFTWARE QUALITY AND SOFTWARE QUALITY MODELS ISO 9126

Software quality refers to the degree to which a software product meets specified requirements, performs its intended functions efficiently, and is free from defects. It is evaluated based on key attributes such as functionality, reliability, usability, efficiency, maintainability, and portability.

A widely accepted framework for defining software quality is the ISO 9126 model, which categorizes software quality into six main characteristics:

- **Functionality** is to ensures the software meets user requirements and performs the intended tasks correctly.
- **Reliability** is to measures the ability of the software to function without failure over time.
- **Usability** assesses how easy and intuitive the software is for users to operate.
- **Efficiency** evaluates the software's performance in terms of speed and resource utilization.
- **Maintainability** determines how easily the software can be modified, updated, and debugged.
- **Portability** checks if the software can function across different platforms and environments.

Software quality is not only about eliminating defects but also about ensuring that the software is scalable, secure, and meets customer expectations. It involves adherence to coding standards, rigorous testing, and continuous improvement processes to ensure a high-quality product that remains reliable and user-friendly.

The **ISO 9126 model** is an international standard for evaluating software quality. It defines software quality based on **six key characteristics**, each further divided into sub-characteristics that help assess the overall quality of a software product:

- Functionality
- Reliability
- Usability
- Efficiency
- Maintainability
- Portability

These characteristics are broken down into sub characteristics, a high-level table is shown below. It is at the sub characteristic level that measurement for SPI will occur. The main characteristics of the ISO9126–1 quality model, can be defined as follows:

1. Functionality

Functionality is the essential purpose of any product or service. For certain items this is relatively easy to define, for example a ship's anchor has the function of holding a ship at a given location. The more functions a product has, e.g. an ATM machine, then the more complicated it becomes to define its functionality. For software a list of functions can be specified, i.e. a sales order processing systems should be able to record customer information so that it can be used to reference a sales order. A sales order system should also provide the following functions:

- Record sales order product, price and quantity.
- Calculate total price.
- Calculate appropriate sales tax.
- Calculate date available to ship, based on inventory.
- Generate purchase orders when stock falls below a given threshold.

The list goes on and on but the main point to note is that functionality is expressed as a totality of essential functions that the software product provides. It is also important to note that the presence or absence of these functions in a software product can be verified as either existing or not, in that it is a Boolean (either a yes or no answer). The other software characteristics listed (i.e. usability) are only present to some degree, i.e. not a simple on or off. Many people get confused between overall process functionality (in which software plays a part) and software functionality. This is partly due to the fact that Data Flow Diagrams (DFDs) and other modeling tools can depict process functionality (as a set of data in\data out conversions) and software functionality. Consider a sales order process, that has both manual and software components. A function of the sales order process could be to record the sales order but we could implement a hard copy filing cabinet for the actual orders and only use software for calculating the price, tax and ship date. In this way the functionality of the software is limited to those calculation functions. SPI, or Software Process Improvement is different from overall Process Improvement or Process Re-engineering, ISO 9126–1 and other software quality models do not help measure overall Process costs\benefits but only the software component. Following functionality, there are 5 other software attributes that characterize the usefulness of the software in a given environment. Each of the following characteristics can only be measured (and are assumed to exist) when the functionality of a given system is present. In this way, for example, a system cannot possess usability characteristics if the system does not function correctly (the two just don't go together).

2. Reliability

Once a software system is functioning, as specified, and delivered the reliability characteristic defines the capability of the system to maintain its service provision under defined conditions for defined periods of time. One aspect of this characteristic is fault tolerance that is the ability of a system to withstand component failure. For example if the network goes down for 20 seconds then comes back the system should be able to recover and continue functioning.

3. Usability

Usability only exists with regard to functionality and refers to the ease of use for a given function. For example a function of an ATM machine is to dispense cash as requested. Placing common amounts on the screen for selection, i.e. $20.00, $40.00, $100.00 etc., does not impact the function of the ATM but addresses the Usability of the function. The ability to learn how to use a system (learnability) is also a major subcharacteristic of usability.

4. Efficiency

This characteristic is concerned with the system resources used when providing the required functionality. The amount of disk space, memory, network etc. provides a good indication of this characteristic. As with a number of these characteristics, there are overlaps. For example the usability of a system is influenced by the system's Performance, in that if a system takes 3 hours to respond the system would not be easy to use although the essential issue is a performance or efficiency characteristic.

5. Maintainability

The ability to identify and fix a fault within a software component is what the maintainability characteristic addresses. In other software quality models this characteristic is referenced as supportability. Maintainability is impacted by code readability or complexity as well as modularization.

Anything that helps with identifying the cause of a fault and then fixing the fault is the concern of maintainability. Also, the ability to verify (or test) a system, i.e. testability, is one of the sub characteristics of maintainability.

6. Portability

This characteristic refers to how well the software can adopt to changes in its environment or with its requirements. The sub characteristics of this characteristic include adaptability. Object oriented design and implementation practices can contribute to the extent to which this characteristic is present in a given system.

Importance of ISO 9126 in Software Quality Management

Helps in systematic evaluation of software quality attributes. Ensures that software meets functional, security, and performance requirements. Supports organizations in developing, testing, and maintaining software efficiently. Enhances customer satisfaction by providing high-quality, reliable products. Provides a foundation for quality assurance and process improvement.

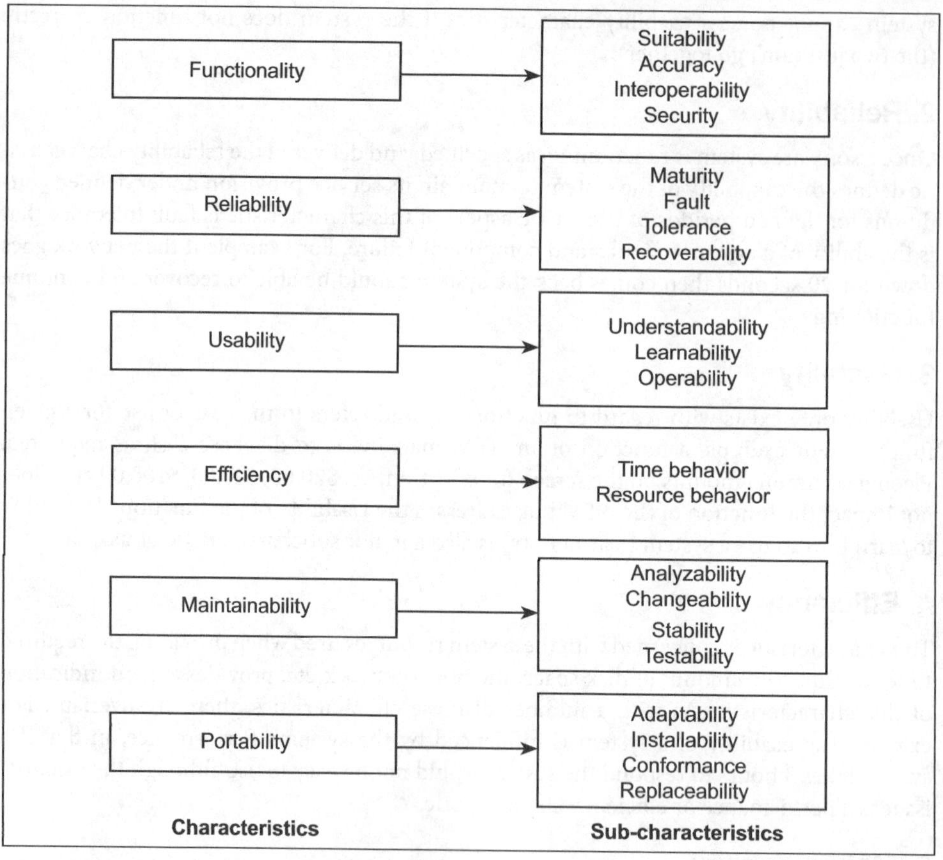

Figure 5.2.

5.4 PRODUCT AND PROCESS METRICS

Software development process metrics can fall into one of the following categories:

- Software process quality metrics.
- Software process timetable metrics.
- Error removal effectiveness metrics.
- Software process productivity metrics.

Software Process Quality Metrics

Software process quality metrics may be classified into two classes:

- Error density metrics.
- Error severity metrics.

Another group of indirect metrics that relates to software process quality is the McCabe's cyclomatic complexity metrics.

Error Density Metrics

Calculation of error density metrics involves two measures: (1) software volume, and (2) errors counted.

Software Volume Measures

Some density metrics use the number of lines of code while others apply function points.

Errors Counted Measures

Some relate to the number of errors and others to the weighted number of errors. Weighted measures that ascertain the severity of the errors are considered to provide more accurate evaluation of the error situation. A common method applied to arrive at this measure is classification of the detected errors into severity classes, followed by weighting each class. The weighted error measure is computed by summing up multiples of the number of errors found in each severity class by the adequate relative severity weight.

Example 1.

This example demonstrates the calculation of the number of code errors (NCE) and the weighted number of code errors (WCE). A soft-ware development department applies two alternative measures, NCE and WCE, to the code errors detected in its software development projects. Three classes of error severity and their relative weights are also defined:

Error severity class	Relative weight
Low severity	1
Medium severity	3
High severity	9

The code error summary for the department's Atlantis project indicated that there were 42 low severity errors, 17 medium severity errors, and 11 high severity errors. Calculation of NCE and WCE gave these results:

	Calculation of NCE	Calculation of WCE	
Error severity class	(number of errors)	Relative weight	Weighted errors
A	*b*	*c*	*d* = *b* x *c*
Low severity	42	1	42
Medium severity	17	3	51
High severity	11	9	99
Total	70	—	192
NCE	70	—	—
WCE	—	—	192

Six Error Density Metrics

- NCE = number of code errors detected in the software code by code inspections and testing. Data for this measure are culled from code inspection and testing reports.
- KLOC = thousands of lines of code.

- NDE = total number of development (design and code) errors detected in the software development process. Data for this measure are found in the various design and code reviews and testing reports conducted.
- WCE = weighted code errors detected. The sources of data for this metric are the same as those for NCE.
- WDE = total weighted development (design and code) errors detected in development of the software. The sources of data for this metric are the same as those for NDE.
- NFP = number of function points required for development of the software. Sources for the number of function points are professional surveys of the relevant software.

CED	Code error density = NCE/KLOC
DED	Development Error Density= NDE/KLOC
WCED	Weighted Code Error Density = WCE/KLOC
WDED	Weighted Development Error Density = WDE/KLOC
WCEF	Weighted Code Errors per Function point = WCE/NFP
WDEF	Weighted Development Errors per Function point = WDE/NFP

Example 2.

This example follows Example 1 and introduces the factor of weighted measures so as to demonstrate the implications of their use. A software development department applies two alternative metrics for calculation of code error density: CED and WCED. The unit determined the following indicators for unacceptable software quality: CED > 2 and WCED > 4. For our calculations we apply the three classes of quality and their relative weights and the code error summary for the Atlantis project mentioned in Example 1. The software system size is 40 KLOC. Calculation of the two metrics resulted in the following:

	Calculation of CED	**Calculation of WCED**
Measures and metrics	**(Code Error Density)**	**(Weighted Code Error Density)**
NCE	70	—
WCE	—	192
KLOC	40	40
CED (NCE/KLOC)	1.75	—
WCED (WCE/KLOC)	—	4.8

The conclusions reached after application of the unweighted versus weighted metrics are different. While the CED *does not* indicate quality *below* the acceptable level, the WCED metric *does* indicate quality *below* the acceptable level (in other words, if the error density is too high, the unit's quality is not acceptable), a result that calls for management intervention.

Error Severity Metrics

The metrics belonging to this group are used to detect adverse situations of increasing numbers of severe errors in situations where errors and weighted errors, as measured by error density metrics, are generally decreasing. Two error severity metrics are presented in below Table:

Error severity metrics		
Code	**Name**	**Calculation formula**
ASCE	Average Severity of Code Errors	ASCE = WCE/NCE
ASDE	Average Severity of Development Errors	ASDE = WDE/NDE

Software Process Timetable Metrics

Software process timetable metrics may be based on accounts of success (completion of milestones per schedule) in addition to failure events (non-completion per schedule). An alternative approach calculates the average delay in completion of milestones. The metrics presented here are based on the two approaches illustrated in the below Table.

Code	Name	Calculation formula
TTO	Time Table Observance	TTO = MSOT/MS
ADMC	Average Delay of Milestone Completion	ADMC = TCDAM/MS

Key

MSOT = milestones completed on time. MS = total number of milestones. TCDAM = total Completion Delays (days, weeks, etc.) for All Milestones. To calculate this measure, delays reported for all relevant milestones are summed up. Milestones completed on time or before schedule are considered "O" delays. Some professionals refer to completion of milestones before schedule as "minus" delays. Error removal effectiveness metrics

Software developers can measure the effectiveness of error removal by the software quality assurance system after a period of regular operation (usually 6 or 12 months) of the system. The metrics combine the error records of the development stage with the failures records compiled during the first year (or any defined period) of regular operation. Two error removal effectiveness metrics are presented in Table.

Code	Name	Calculation formula
DERE	Development Errors Removal Effectiveness	DERE = NDE/ (NDE+NYF)
DWERE	Development Weighted Errors Removal Effectiveness	DWERE = WDE/ (WDE+WYF)

Key

- NYF = number of software failures detected during a year of maintenance service.
- WYF = weighted number of software failures detected during a year of maintenance service.

Software Process Productivity Metrics

This group of metrics includes "direct" metrics that deal with a project's human resources productivity as well as "indirect" metrics that focus on the extent of software reuse. Software reuse substantially affects productivity and effectiveness. Four process productivity metrics, direct and indirect, are presented in Table:

Code	Name	Calculation formula
DevP	Development Productivity	DeVH/KLOC
FDevP	Function point Development Productivity	DeVH/NFP
CRe	Code Reuse	ReKLOC/KLOC
DocRe	Documentation Reuse	ReDOC/NDoc

Key

- DevH = total working hours invested in the development of the software system.
- ReKLOC = number of thousands of reused lines of code.
- ReDoc = number of reused pages of documentation.
- NDoc = number of pages of documentation.

Product Metrics

Product metrics refer to the software system's operational phase – years of regular use of the software system by customers, whether "internal" or "external" customers, who either purchased the software system or contracted for its development. In most cases, the software developer is required to provide customer service during the software's operational phase. *Customer services are of two main types:*

- **Help desk services HD:** software support by instructing customers regarding the method of application of the software and solution of customer implementation problems. Demand for these services depends to a great extent on the quality of the user interface (its "user friendliness") as well as the quality of the user manual and integrated help menus.
- **Corrective maintenance services:** correction of software failures identified by customers/users or detected by the customer service team prior to their discovery by customers. The number of software failures and their density are directly related to software development quality. For completeness of information and better control of failure correction, it is recommended that all software failures detected by the customer service team be recorded as corrective maintenance calls.

HD metrics are based on all customer calls while corrective maintenance metrics are based on failure reports. Product metrics generally rely on performance records compiled during one year (or any other specified period of time). This policy enables comparisons of successive years in addition to comparisons between different units and software systems.

The array of software product metrics presented here is classified as follows:

1. HD quality metrics
2. HD productivity and effectiveness metrics
3. Corrective maintenance quality metrics
4. Corrective maintenance productivity and effectiveness metrics.

1. Hd Quality Metrics

The types of HD quality metrics are:

- HD calls density metrics – the extent of customer requests for HD services as measured by the number of calls.

- Metrics of the severity of the HD issues raised.
- HD success metrics – the level of success in responding to these calls. A success is achieved by completing the required service within the time determined in the service contract.

Hd Calls Density Metrics

This section describes six different types of metrics. Some relate to the number of the errors and others to a weighted number of errors. As for size/volume measures of the software, some use number of lines of code while others apply function points. The sources of data for these and the other metrics in this group are HD reports. Three HD calls density metrics for HD performance are presented in Table.

Code	Name	Calculation formula
HDD	HD calls Density	NHYC/KLMC
WHDD	Weighted HD calls Density	WHYC/KLMC
WHDF	Weighted HD calls per Function point	WHYC/NMFP

Key

- NHYC = number of HD calls during a year of service.

  KLMC = thousands of lines of maintained software code.
- WHYC = weighted HD calls received during one year of service.

  NMFP = number of function points to be maintained.

Success of the HD services

The most common metric for the success of HD services is the capacity to solve problems raised by customer calls within the time determined in the service contract (*availability*). Thus, the metric for success of HD services compares the actual with the designated time for provision of these services.

For example, the availability of help desk (HD) services for an inventory management software package is defined as follows:

- The HD service undertakes to solve any HD call within one hour.
- The probability that HD call solution time exceeds one hour will not exceed 2%.
- The probability that HD call solution time exceeds four working hours will not exceed 0.5%.

2. HD Productivity and Effectiveness Metrics

Productivity metrics relate to the total of resources invested during a specified period, while effectiveness metrics relate to the resources invested in responding to a HD customer call.

HD Productivity Metrics

HD productivity metrics makes use of the easy-to-apply KLMC measure of maintained software system's size or according to function-point evaluation of the software system. Two HD productivity metrics are presented in Table.

Code	Name	Calculation formula
HDP	HD Productivity	HDP = HDYH/KLMC
FHDP	Function point HD Productivity	FHDP = HDYH/NMFP

Key

- HDYH = total yearly working hours invested in HD servicing of the software system.
- HD effectiveness metrics

The metrics in this group refer to the resources invested in responding to customers' HD calls.

3. Corrective Maintenance Quality Metrics

Software corrective maintenance metrics deal with several aspects of the quality of maintenance services. A distinction is needed between software system failures treated by the maintenance teams and failures of the maintenance service that refer to cases where the maintenance failed to provide a repair that meets the designated standards or contract requirements. Thus, software maintenance metrics are classified as follows:

Software system failures density metrics deal with the extent of demand for corrective maintenance, based on the records of failures identified during regular operation of the software system.

Software system failures severity metrics – deal with the severity of soft-ware system failures attended to by the corrective maintenance team.

Failures of maintenance services metrics deal with cases where maintenance services were unable to complete the failure correction on time or that the correction performed failed. Software system availability metrics – deal with the extent of disturbances caused to the customer as realized by periods of time where the services of the software system are unavailable or only partly available.

Software System Failures Density Metrics

The software system failures density metrics presented here relate to the number and/or weighted number of failures. The size of the maintenance tasks is measured by the total number of code lines of the maintained software as well as by the function point evaluation. The sources of data for these metrics are software maintenance reports. Three software system failures density metrics are presented in Table.

Code	Name	Calculation formula
SSFD	Software System Failure Density	NYF/KLMC
WSSFD	Weighted Software System Failure Density	WYF/KLMC
WSSFF	Weighted Software System Failures per Function point	WYF/NMFP

Key

- NYF = number of software failures detected during a year of maintenance service.
- WYF = weighted number of yearly software failures detected during a year of maintenance service.

- KLMC = thousands of lines of maintained software code.
- NMFP = number of function points designated for the maintained software.

Software System Failures Severity Metrics

Metrics of this group detect adverse situations of increasingly severe failures in the maintained software. Results may trigger retesting of all or parts of the software system. The events measured relate either to the disturbances and damages caused to the customer (representing the customer's point of view) or to the resources required to resolve the failure (representing the interests of the maintenance team).

Severity of Software System Failures (ASSSF) = WYF/NYF

Key

- NYF = number of software failures detected during a year of maintenance service.
- WYF = weighted number of yearly software failures detected during a year of maintenance service.

Failures of Maintenance Services Metrics

Maintenance services can fail either because they were unable to complete the failure correction on time or when the correction per-formed failed and a repeated correction is required.

Maintenance Repeated repair Failure (MRepF) = RepYF/NYF

where RepYF is the number of repeated software failure calls (service failures).

Software System Availability Metrics

User metrics distinguish between:

- Full availability – where all software system functions perform properly
- Vital availability – where no vital functions fail (but non-vital functions may fail)
- Total unavailability – where all software system functions fail.
    - FA = (NYSerH-NYFH)/NYSerH
    - NYSerH = number of hours software system is in service during one year.
    - NYFH = number of hours where at least one function is unavailable (failed) during one year, including total failure of the software system.

4. Software Corrective Maintenance Productivity and Effectiveness Metrics

While corrective maintenance productivity relates to the total of human resources invested in maintaining a given software system, corrective maintenance effectiveness relates to the resources invested in correction of a single failure. In other words, a software maintenance system displaying higher productivity will require fewer resources for its maintenance task, while a more effective software maintenance system will require fewer resources, on average, for correcting one failure.

CMaiP = Corrective Maintenance Productivity = CMaiYH/KLMC

Where

CMaiYH = total yearly working hours invested in the corrective maintenance of the software system.

KLMC = thousands of lines of maintained software code.

5.5 PRODUCT VERSUS PROCESS QUALITY MANAGEMENT

When considering the maintenance contract, a broad perspective should be embraced. More than anything else, decisions are required about the categories of services to be contracted. These decisions depend on the type of customers served: customers for whom a custom-made package has been developed, customers who purchased a COTS software package, and internal customers. So, before commencing to supply software maintenance services to any of these customers, an adequate maintenance contract should be finalized that sets down the total range of maintenance obligations according to the relevant conditions.

A fundamental assumption of quality management is that the quality of the development process directly affects the quality of the delivered products The link between software process quality and software product quality is complex Process quality management involves defining process standards such as how and when reviews should be conducted monitoring the development process to ensure that the standards are being followed reporting the software process to project management and to the buyer of the software

5.6 QUALITY MANAGEMENT SYSTEMS

Planning software quality involves defining the required product in terms of its quality (internal and external) characteristics Planning the processes to achieve the required product Characteristics that govern how the product works in its environment are called external, which include, for example, usability and reliability Characteristic related to how the product was developed are called internal quality characteristics, and include, for example, structural complexity, size, test coverage, and fault rates. Quality assurance process: ensuring that the software products and processes in the project life cycle conform to their specified requirements by planning, enacting, and performing a set of activities to provide adequate confidence that the quality is being built into the software Verification and validation processes: assessing software products throughout the product life cycle Review and audit processes: involving Management reviews, technical reviews, Inspections, Walk through and Audits.

Quality Planning

Quality planning is the process of developing a quality plan for the project. A quality plan involves

- **Product Introduction:** A description of the product, its intended market and the quality expectation for the product
- **Product plans:** The critical release dates and responsibilities for the product along with plans for distribution and product servicing
- **Process descriptions:** the development and service processes that should be used for product development and management
- **Quality Goals:** The quality goals and plans for the product including an identification and justification of critical product quality attributes

- **Risks and risk management:** The key risks that might affect product quality and the actions to address these risks Quality Assurance and Standards is the process of defining how software quality can be achieved and how the development organization knows that the software has the required level of quality Quality assurance standards Product standards, Product standards Software standards are based on knowledge ("best-practice" or "state-of-the-art") provide a framework for implementing a quality assurance process to assist/support continuity in practice within an organization Issues: Software engineers sometimes dislike standards need to involve software engineering in the selection of standards review and modify standards regularly to reflect changing technologies to provide software tools to support standards where possible.

5.7 PROCESS CAPABILITY MODELS

Process capability models are frameworks used to assess, measure, and improve software development processes to enhance software quality. These models help organizations identify strengths and weaknesses in their processes and establish systematic improvements for higher efficiency, reliability, and maintainability.

Key Process Capability Models

Capability Maturity Model Integration (CMMI)

A widely used framework that defines five levels of process maturity:

Level 1: Initial – Unpredictable and reactive processes.

Level 2: Managed – Basic project management is in place.

Level 3: Defined – Organization-wide standardization of processes.

Level 4: Quantitatively Managed – Processes are measured and controlled.

Level 5: Optimizing – Continuous improvement through feedback and innovation.

ISO/IEC 15504 (SPICE - Software Process Improvement and Capability Determination)

A model for evaluating software development processes based on capability levels. Defines a six-level scale from Level 0 (Incomplete) to Level 5 (Optimizing). Helps organizations assess and improve process effectiveness and compliance.

Six Sigma

A methodology aimed at reducing defects and variations in software processes. Uses DMAIC (Define, Measure, Analyze, Improve, Control) to enhance process quality. Focuses on data-driven decision-making and continuous process improvements. Lean Software Development focuses on eliminating waste, improving efficiency, and delivering value faster. Based on seven principles, including continuous improvement and customer focus. Helps streamline software development by reducing delays and unnecessary work.

Importance of Process Capability Models in Software Quality

Standardizes software development processes to improve consistency and efficiency. Reduces defects and failures, leading to higher software reliability. Enhances maintainability and scalability of software products. Improves project management through structured methodologies. Boosts customer satisfaction by delivering high-quality, well-tested software.

5.8 TECHNIQUES TO HELP ENHANCE SOFTWARE QUALITY

One of the important issues that business has focused on in the last two decades is "quality". The other issues are cost and delivery. Quality has been widely considered as a key element for success in business in the present competitive market. Quality refers to meeting the needs and expectations of customers. It is important to understand that quality is about more than a product simply working properly. Quality refers to certain standards and the ways and means by which those standards are achieved, maintained and improved. Quality is not just confined to products and services. It is a homogeneous element of any aspect of doing things with high degree of perfection.

For example, Business success depends on the quality decision making.

Quality control: series of inspections, reviews, and tests used to ensure conformance of a work product (artifact) to its specifications.

Quality assurance: auditing and reporting procedures used to provide management with data needed to make proactive decisions The following factors are used by customers when evaluating quality of software:

1. **Correctness:** A software product is correct, if different requirements as specified in the SRS document have been correctly implemented. (Accuracy of result)
2. **Portability:** A software product is said to be portable, if it can be easily made to work in different operating systems, in different machines, with other software products, etc.
3. **Reusability:** A software product has good reusability, if different modules of the product can easily be reused to develop new products.
4. **Usability:** A software product has good usability, if different categories of users (i.e. both expert and novice users) can easily invoke the functions of the product.
5. **Maintainability:** A software product is maintainable, if errors can be easily corrected as and when they show up, new functions can be easily added to the product, functionalities of the product can be easily modified, etc.
6. **Tangibility:** Appearance of physical facilities, equipment, personnel and communication materials.
7. **Empathy:** Caring, Individualized attention the firm provides its customers.
8. **Responsiveness:** Willingness to help customers and provide prompt service.
9. **Assurance:** Knowledge and courtesy of employees and their ability to convey trust and confidence.
10. **Efficiency:** Efficiency is a factor relating to all issues in the execution of software; it includes considerations such as response time, memory requirement, and throughput.

5.9 TESTING AND SOFTWARE RELIABILITY

Software tests are formal SQA components that are targeted toward review of the actual running of the software. The tests are based on a prepared list of test cases that represent a variety of expected scenarios. Software tests examine software modules, software integration, or entire software packages (systems). Recurrent tests (usually termed "regression tests"), carried out after correction of previous test findings, are continued till satisfactory results are obtained.

Software testing programs are constructed from a variety of tests, some manual and some automated. All tests have to be designed, planned and approved according to development procedures. The test report will include a detailed list of the faults detected and recommendations about the performance of partial or complete recurrent tests following a subsequent round of corrections based on the test findings.

It is recommended that software tests be carried out by an independent, outside testing unit rather than by the project team, as the project team will naturally find it difficult to detect faults they failed to detect during development as well as to avoid conflicts of interest.

Quality assurance procedures usually provide detailed definitions for the performance of specific types of development activities in a way that assures effective achievement of quality results. Work instructions, in contrast, provide detailed directions for the use of methods that are applied in unique instances and employed by specialized teams.

Procedures and work instructions are based on the organization's accumulated experience and knowledge; as such, they contribute to the correct and effective performance of established technologies and routines. Because they reflect the organization's past experience, constant care should be taken to update and adjust those procedures and instructions to current technological, organizational, and other conditions.

5.10 QUALITY PLANS

Planning is meant to prepare adequate foundations for successful and timely completion of the project.

The planning process includes:

1. Scheduling development activities and estimating the required manpower resources and budget
2. Recruiting team members and allocating development resources
3. Resolving development risks
4. Implementing required SQA activities
5. Providing management with data needed for project control

Elements of The Development Plan

The project's development plan is prepared to fulfill the above objectives. The following elements, each applicable to different project components, comprise a project development plan.

Project Products

The development plan includes the following products: Design documents specifying dates of completion, indicating those items to be delivered to the customer ("deliverables") Software products (specifying completion date and installation site) Training tasks (specifying dates, participants and sites).

Project Interfaces

Project interfaces include Interfaces with existing software packages (software interface) Interfaces with other software and/or hardware development teams that are working on the same system or project (i.e., cooperation and coordination links) Interfaces with existing hardware (hardware interface). Project methodology and development tools to be applied at each phase of the project. Never use untested tool/methodology on a new project with high visibility.

Software Development Standards and Procedures

A list should be prepared of the software development standards and procedures to be applied in the project.

The Mapping of the Development Process

Mapping of the development process involves providing detailed definitions of each of the project's phases. These descriptions include definitions of inputs and outputs, and the specific activities planned.

Activity descriptions include:

(a) An estimate of the activity's duration. These estimates are highly dependent on the experience gained in previous projects.

(b) The logical sequence in which each activity is to be performed, including a description of each activity's dependence on previously completed activities.

(c) The type of professional resources required and estimates of how much of these resources are necessary for each activity.

Several methods are available for scheduling and graphically presenting the development process. One of the most commonly used methods is the GANTT chart, which displays the various activities by horizontal bars whose lengths are proportional to the activity's duration.

Project Milestones

- Completion dates, products clearly define.
- Must synchronize with Overall Plan.
- More detailed than Overall Plan.
- More detailed than iteration plans.

Project Staff Organization

The organization plan comprises:

Organizational structure: definition of project teams and their tasks, including teams comprised of a subcontractor's temporary workers.

Professional requirements: professional certification, experience in a specific programming language or development tool, experience with a specific software product and type, and so forth. Number of team members required for each period of time, according to the activities scheduled. It is expected that teams will commence their activities at different times, and that their team size may vary from one period to the next, depending on the planned activities.

Names of team leaders and team members. Difficulties are expected to arise with respect to the long-term assignment of staff members to teams because of unanticipated changes in their current assignments. Therefore, the names of staff are required to help keep track of their participation as team members.

Development Facilities

Required development facilities include hardware, software and hardware development tools, office space, and other items. Nowadays very nice facilities are provided by organization- break rooms, nice coffee shop, day care.

Development Risks

A development risk is "a state or property of a development task or environment, which, if ignored, will increase the likelihood of project failure". Typical development risks are:

- **Technological gaps:** Lack of adequate and sufficient professional knowledge and experience to carry out the demands of the development contract.
- **Staff shortages:** Unanticipated shortfalls of professional staff. Interdependence of **organizational elements:** The likelihood that suppliers of specialized hardware or software subcontractors, for example, will not fulfill their obligations on schedule.

Control Method

In order to control project implementation, the project manager and the department management apply a series of monitoring practices when preparing progress reports and coordinating meetings.

Elements of The Quality Plan

List of Quality Goals

These refer to the quality requirements in the developed software system. Quantitative measures usually preferred to qualitative measures when choosing goals because they are usually easier to assess objectively during testing. Quality goals should reflect the major acceptance criteria found in the requirement's document - correctness, reliability, robustness, maintainability. RFP is often used to measure successful achievement of the customer's quality requirements.

Planned Review Activities

The planned reviews should include a listing of all reviews.

- design reviews
- technical reviews
- managerial reviews
- code inspections
- Pros and Cons

Planned Software Tests

The quality plan should provide a complete list of planned software tests, with the following designated for each test. The unit, integration or the complete system to be tested. The type of testing activities to be carried out, including specification of computerized software tests to be applied. The planned test schedule (as defined by its priority and the succeeding activities of the project process)

Planned Acceptance Tests for Externally Developed Software

A complete set of acceptance tests to be run for externally developed software must be provided within the quality plan.

Configuration Management

The quality plan must include configuration management tools and procedures for managing the software configurations, versions, etc. The Quality Plan may be included within the Development Plan or as an independent document.

UNIT SUMMARY

Software quality ensures that a software product meets user requirements, functions correctly, and remains free of defects. The importance of software quality lies in its ability to enhance user satisfaction, reduce maintenance costs, and improve security and performance. Defining software quality involves standardized models like ISO 9126, which categorizes quality into attributes such as functionality, reliability, usability, efficiency, maintainability, and portability. To measure quality, product and process metrics are used, where product metrics assess aspects like performance and complexity, while process metrics evaluate development efficiency. The distinction between product and process quality management highlights the need to focus not only on the final product but also on optimizing the development process. A strong focus on software quality leads to reliable, efficient, and user-friendly products while minimizing defects and long-term costs.

EXERCISES

1. What is software quality, and why is it important?
2. Define ISO 9126 and explain its key quality attributes.
3. How do product metrics differ from process metrics?
4. What is the difference between product quality and process quality management?
5. What are the main functions of a Quality Management System (QMS)?
6. How does a process capability model like CMMI help improve software development?
7. Name three techniques used to enhance software quality and briefly explain them.
8. Why is software testing crucial for ensuring reliability?
9. What are some common types of software testing used in quality assurance?
10. What key elements should be included in a software quality plan?

UUU